"I recommend *The Value Equation* for all investors, as the author, Chris Volk, provides readers with all of the ingredients for a successful and profitable business. His expertise in credit and financial underwriting is a key differentiator that makes this author outstanding in his field. As a shareholder in STORE Capital, I have followed Volk's journey for over a decade, and I can't wait to see what's in 'store' for him now. I have a feeling it will have something to do with creating wealth via 'the value equation'. Well done Mr. Volk!

Brad Thomas, *CEO of Wide Moat Research*

The Value Equation

A Business Guide to Wealth Creation for Entrepreneurs, Leaders & Investors

by
Christopher H. Volk

WILEY

For general information on our other products and services or for technical support, please contact our Customer Care Department within the United States at (800) 762-2974, outside the United States at (317) 572-3993 or fax (317) 572-4002.

Wiley also publishes its books in a variety of electronic formats. Some content that appears in print may not be available in electronic formats. For more information about Wiley products, visit our website at www.wiley.com.

Library of Congress Cataloging-in-Publication Data:

Names: Volk, Christopher H., author.
Title: The value equation : a business guide to wealth creation for
    entrepreneurs, leaders & investors / Christopher H. Volk.
Description: Hoboken, NJ : Wiley, [2022] | Includes index.
Identifiers: LCCN 2022002736 (print) | LCCN 2022002737 (ebook) | ISBN
    9781119875642 (cloth) | ISBN 9781119875666 (adobe pdf) | ISBN
    9781119875659 (epub)
Subjects: LCSH: Corporations—Valuation. | Business planning. | Wealth.
Classification: LCC HG4028.V3 V64 2022 (print) | LCC HG4028.V3 (ebook) |
    DDC 658.15—dc23/eng/20220301
LC record available at https://lccn.loc.gov/2022002736
LC ebook record available at https://lccn.loc.gov/2022002737

Cover Design and Image: © Classic Sky LLC
SKY10033121_032322

For my wife,
the love of my life,
who makes so much possible.

Contents

Preface

I did not initially set out to be an entrepreneur. I graduated from college in the middle of a major economic recession with a mediocre grade point average, having avoided taking a single business class. It was then that something fortunate happened to me that would guide my future choices: My applications for employment were declined by more than 300 companies.

Getting rejected by so many businesses was an accomplishment in 1979. Each letter I sent went by regular mail and was hand typed. So were the replies. For years, I kept the rejection letters as a reminder of the privilege of employment. Those letters also provided me with added motivation to succeed. With my mounting rejections, I would likely have taken any reasonable offer of employment at just about any location. Fortunately, the rejections deprived me of that opportunity and gave me time to think.

I committed to a course of action, narrowing my focus. I decided to convince a commercial bank to hire me. The idea was to maintain my career options while finding a job that would give me valuable knowledge about business and finance. I also attended night school, eventually earning an MBA. My brief banking career led me to finance and eventually to the opportunity to take three companies public on the New York Stock Exchange, two of which I co-founded. All the while, I have been a student and observer of business.

This book has been years in the making. It began with many published articles written throughout my career that eventually provided the material for an award-winning video series on business. In turn, the video series was inspired by an educational program called *Schoolhouse Rock!* When I was in high school, it was brilliantly conceived to make many complex subjects simple. I wanted to do something like that for business, using math you learned in middle school.

This book ultimately emerged from that effort.

Corporate business models cannot be conceived or evaluated without math. Over my career, I have found that most businesspeople are taught to look at absolute numbers. The approach within this book is intended to be broadly accessible and is centered instead on universal relative numeric relationships, beginning with investor rates of return. In taking this approach, which I have used throughout my career, complex business models can be hugely simplified. For you, the result is that a wide range of business financial fundamentals can be addressed using a single integrated approach and then condensed into a few pages.

When you are done reading this book, you should have more than just a basic understanding of how businesses create wealth. You can expect to have a good idea how companies are assembled and valued. And you will also gain insight into how business leaders work to improve corporate business models in ways that generate personal and collective wealth. These fundamentals rest at the heart of the creation of most of the largest personal fortunes ever assembled.

Businesses lie in the middle of the great river of global commerce. They are the engine of our global economy and are ultimately responsible for our collective prosperity. I have spent a career in the middle of the river and am happy to be able to share my observations with you. This book contains many illustrations of businesses, including STORE Capital, the most recent publicly traded company I co-founded.

The business case study illustrations within the book generally stop at 2019. The reasoning should be intuitive. The global pandemic that began in early 2020 created major global disruptions that resulted in near-term business performance and business model distortions. Given the timeless nature of the concepts in this book, this does not matter.

I have been fortunate to work in a time characterized by a high level of business formation and creativity, which has helped me and many others start large businesses from scratch. To my knowledge, business formation has never been more accessible. It is my hope that this book serves to inspire readers to harness the wealth creation potential of business as they contribute to, create, and run businesses that benefit us all.

Christopher Volk
Paradise Valley, Arizona
March 18, 2022

Introduction

There are many ways to get rich. Strategies for personal wealth creation often center on personal habits that encourage controlled spending, the avoidance of debt, and the accumulation of investment assets designed to make your money work for you. But there is far less written about how *businesses create wealth*. I went through two years of graduate business school and emerged without taking a single class on the subject. Nor have I noticed any significant change in the understanding of business students in the intervening years since.

Corporate wealth creation stands at the center of our national economic prosperity. Most of us work for businesses. And it turns out, the richest among us did more than simply control spending, avoid debt, and accumulate investment assets. The very wealthiest Americans either made their money by owning a business or by inheriting money from family members who did. The investment assets they accumulated were centered in their own business endeavors.

Any discussion of business is incomplete without a discussion of wealth creation. The two go hand in hand, like peanut butter and jelly. Most growing business enterprises need independent investor capital, and a prerequisite for attracting investors is the company's potential for wealth creation. If a business is unlikely to be worth more than it cost to create—either now or in the near future—it is equally unlikely to attract the independent investor capital it needs.

And therein is the definition of business wealth creation: Making a business worth more than it cost to create.

To make something become worth more than it cost to create involves being an active investor. Investing in public stocks or bonds can deliver returns that can make you rich over time, but those returns are generally part of the fabric of overall corporate costs of capital. Businesses are *supposed* to reward you for making an investment in their stocks or bonds. Every now and again, investments in public stocks are rewarded with outsized returns as some of the business wealth created by leadership is sprinkled onto shareholders. Every now and again, investments in public stocks will be rewarded with outsized returns as investors pan for gold, seeking undervalued companies having solid, but misunderstood, business models. But corporate wealth creation tends to fall disproportionately on the corporate founders and early investors who took the risk. They are the first to be rewarded for making the company worth more than the cost of its parts.

Businesses have many stakeholders, including their investors. Those many stakeholders include owners, employees, creditors, suppliers, and communities. Today, one can be overwhelmed by the flood of published books and articles that debate which stakeholders are owed the highest degree of loyalty. To analyze the relative importance of stakeholder constituencies is easiest with established businesses, especially if they have grown to be large and powerful. But no large business I can think of got to be that way without first having created massive amounts of wealth for its founding owners. Without the strong potential for wealth creation, such companies would never have existed.

People who put their money into a start-up business typically have other investment choices. Those choices generally come with investment return expectations. In turn, such expectations effectively create a hurdle rate to attract investor capital to a new business. If you can meet or exceed that hurdle rate, then you have a chance to accomplish more than simply earning and saving money. You can create wealth from thin air by making your business worth more than it cost to put in place.

Here is a simple illustration: Since it was first created in 1926, investors in the S&P 500 stock index have earned, on average, 10% annually. That might make 10% the institutional investor benchmark hurdle rate, though I would note that I have generally seen more aggressive investor targets for newly minted companies. The hurdle rate, in this case 10%, is the starting point for wealth creation. Should your business produce a total investor rate of return of 10%, then your company will be simply worth what it cost to create. Raise that delivered return to 20% and your investment doubles in value. In business, it is the *excess return*, and not the appreciation of underlying business assets, which creates value from thin air. Likewise, a business can easily be worth less than what it cost to create. In this case, should your company's total rate of return be a mere 5%, then your investment value would stand to fall in half.

People commonly confuse *investment returns* with *wealth creation*. They are not the same. Think of it: A company could provide its shareholders with a meaty annual rate of return of 10%, yet still have created no value above what it cost to create. In turn, if you accumulate enough investable assets capable of delivering 10% annual rates of return over time, you can personally become rich. But keep in mind that without the potential to deliver annual returns greater than 10%, the company in our example would likely never have been able to attract sophisticated outside investor capital. The independent investors would likely have elected to invest their money elsewhere, possibly into the S&P 500 Index, which is backed by a portfolio of the nation's largest seasoned companies having far greater investment liquidity and far less execution risk.

Most established businesses realize rates of return that are not attractive for outside investors and yet still allow their owners to make a decent living and save some money. But wealth that is created out of thin air can only be achieved in business by producing annual rates of return above applicable return benchmarks. If you can achieve this, then you and your leadership team have realized an enormous accomplishment. If you can achieve this while also satisfying your many other stakeholders, then you can say you have attained a truly rare level of business success.

Shareholder wealth creation is the single most important corporate financial performance metric. It's not that hard to figure out. Just calculate what a company cost to create, then subtract what it owes to creditors, and you get a number equal to what owners have invested at cost. Now, compare that owner investment to its current valuation—this is obviously easiest with a public company—and you arrive at the amount of shareholder wealth creation. This number is called *equity market value added*, or EMVA, which is simply the amount by which a company's shareholder equity is worth more than it cost to create.

Once you know the amount of value creation, you can compute the annual compound growth rate of your EMVA. Key to this computation is knowing the weighted average age of company equity at cost, which will almost always be younger than a company's chronological age. That is because most companies reinvest some or all their free cash flows back into the business, rather than distribute that free cash flow to shareholders. The result is that the cost basis of a company's equity rises each year as company management reinvests shareholder cash flows into the business. In the case of the companies I have helped lead, we have also raised new shareholder capital annually, which has served to further reduce the effective age of our business. Financially speaking, the higher the annual compound EMVA growth you can realize, the better you are.

EMVA growth is a far better long-term business evaluation metric than compound earnings growth. Between 2015 and 2019, Walmart, amongst the most valuable publicly traded companies and the single largest retailer and corporate employer in the US, threw off close to $30 billion annually in free cash flow from operations. The company paid out only about 20% of that in shareholder dividends, which means that about 80% of annual shareholder cash flows were available for reinvestment into the company each year.

Assuming Walmart reinvested the money profitably into its business, how could earnings per share fail to go up? Really, the company could have lit on fire half of its annual retained cash flow, reinvested the other half into earnings-producing investments, and net income per share would be expected to rise.

The reinvestment of cash flows is the main reason that broad stock market indices rise over the long term. They have to. Yet, for shareholders, the paramount issue should be whether companies are able to retain and reinvest their free cash flows without losing any of the value of that reinvested cash. And while not losing any wealth would be great, creating added EMVA would be even better.

Regrettably, too few Americans understand the power and dynamics of business wealth creation. Many of us believe that wealth is beyond our reach and that our market economy is somehow rigged to favor an elite few. I have never believed this. At its heart, America aspires to be a meritocracy. If you are fortunate enough to live in America, your potential should be limited only by your imagination, dedication, and discipline.

My experience is that good ideas, solid business models, and qualified leadership teams are scarcer than the investor capital needed to support and sponsor them. In my career, this has become increasingly true. If you are considering an idea having the potential for wealth creation, America is as good a place as I can think of to execute it. For one, the US, with approximately 4% of the world's population, has more small- and middle-market companies than any other country in the world. According to the US Small Business Administration and the US Census Bureau, as of 2018, there were approximately 26 million small businesses having no paid employees other than the owner, and more than 6 million small businesses with fewer than 500 paid employees. Those small businesses collectively employed nearly half of all working Americans.

The growth of capital availability to fund business ideas is equally impressive. When I graduated from college in 1979, there were scarcely any private equity investment companies. Forty years on, there are no fewer than 10,000 private equity and venture capital firms investing in every kind of company imaginable. Add them all together and you have an abundance of capital unheard of in American history. With a highly open economy and a strong legal framework, both of which are essential to encourage business formation, the US has a veritable conga line of lenders and equity investors in search of solid ideas having wealth creation potential. I learned this personally—access to investment capital enabled me to co-found companies in 2003 and 2011 that would both go on to be listed on the New York Stock Exchange.

Among the greatest gifts my parents gave me were an education and an example. In 1980, with nothing but a college degree in history and French, $500, and a box of hundreds of rejection letters from prospective employers, I loaded up my 1970 Volkswagen in New York and drove to Atlanta, Georgia. I landed a job selling clothing, and then started attending night school to learn about business. A few months later, I was hired by a regional bank—my goal was to work for a bank—where I would spend the next six years. For most of those years, I was engaged analyzing businesses and evaluating their ability to repay loans. I also spent many of my evenings in night school, earning my MBA. Along the way, I learned something that seems obvious: Not all businesses are created equal. Some businesses simply have superior business models that enable greater wealth creation.

Once a year since 1982, *Forbes* magazine has published its list of the 400 richest Americans. With few exceptions, members of this elite listing owe their fortunes to the wealth creation engines of some of the world's finest businesses. The fortunate self-made members of the list followed personal interests, often had luck shine on them, and found themselves owning stakes in groundbreaking businesses they helped create that became worth billions of dollars. In turn, the businesses they created were endowed with some of the finest business models capable of producing gargantuan rates of return that so exceeded any rational investor return expectation that they literally created geysers of wealth from thin air. Often, the wealth created was so abundant that it's common to see multiple members of the Forbes 400 who owe their vast collective net worth to the same singular corporate successes. Importantly, the geysers of created wealth often rained down broadly on employees and investors.

After I started to work at the bank, I became interested in business models. From my earliest days in banking, I began to model out businesses and create projections, which helped me to develop an expertise in business model evaluation. I cut my teeth on Visicalc (the first spreadsheet software for personal computers), graduated to Lotus 123, and later moved on to Excel, which is the prevalent spreadsheet software in use today. My earliest financial models can be described as long and weighty.

The thing about most business models and projections is that they are bound to be *wrong*. In fact, I commonly saw companies put together "base case," "best case," and "worst case" financial model scenarios, which simply gave the model authors the opportunity to be wrong three times. In truth, with just one or two variable changes, business model outcomes can vary by great degrees. Given this high level of variability, I became wedded to sensitivity tables (or "data tables" in Excel), which allowed me to see potential outcomes given a range of values for any two key model inputs. If you created many sensitivity tables, you could incorporate numerous variables, which provided better insight into key model variables and margins for error. The best business models tend to have ample room to make mistakes and yet still create wealth through outsized investor returns.

When we raised the investor money to start STORE Capital in 2011, the financial model I prepared was important. (STORE is an acronym for Single Tenant Operational Real Estate, inspired by our dedication to investment real estate that serves as profit center locations for our many customers.) At the time, I figured that the *worst* we could likely do was to realize an annual rate of shareholder return of around 9%, with an expected annual rate of return closer to 20%. By the time our original founding institutional shareholders sold their shares in the first quarter of 2016, they had realized a compound annual rate of return of approximately 26%.

With many founding corporate investments, the downside is a complete loss of all invested funds. In our case, we believed we could

at least produce an annual rate of return that exceeded the aggregate return requirements of the pension fund capital that seeded
our new business, with substantial upside. In 2011, our plan and an
excellent leadership team allowed us to garner an investor commitment of $500 million to launch STORE Capital. At the time, there
were just five founders with a vision, no offices, no assets, and many
virtual meetings. Two years later, with the company on track, we
accepted another $530 million in investor commitments. Another
year and a half later, we listed STORE Capital on the New York
Stock Exchange. By the end of 2019, STORE had an enterprise valuation approaching $12 billion. More importantly, we had created
more than $3 billion in equity market value added.

Over the years, my approach to financial modeling became simpler. Complex models are neat, but they can be prone to greater
error. If I did a complex model, it was always wise to have a simple model just to see if the results approximated one another. In a
way, financial models are like computer programs: the fewer lines
of code you write, the faster and more dependable the result is. For
Investor Day demonstrations at STORE Capital, I would reduce the
corporate financial model inputs to just 14 key variables. Take that
in for a moment: We had a company having over $9 billion in assets,
annual revenues greater than $600 million, and 95 employees, and
it was possible to whittle our entire enterprise down to 14 variables.

You may be wondering why a discussion of corporate financial
modeling approaches is so important. Well, it turns out that you
can create a basic corporate financial model with as few as six variables that drive investor rates of return. At a high level, this means
that corporate leaders have just these Six Variables—as I've named
them—under their control, all working in concert with one another
to deliver investor rates of return. And, as you should know by now,
potent business models having investor rates of return that exceed
investor return requirements lie at the heart of business wealth
creation. So, the Six Variables work collectively to form a framework for understanding the essentials of how businesses work to
create wealth.

Understanding that framework may make you more interested in business.

Understanding that framework may influence your employment decisions.

Understanding that framework may help you to lead a business.

Understanding that framework might inspire you to start a business.

Understanding this framework will make you a better business investor.

Understanding that framework will improve your personal wealth opportunities.

That's what this book is all about.

Chapter 1

Free Enterprise and Wealth Creation

I n the United States, businesses—large and small, public and private—create the beating heart of individual and national wealth creation. At the end of 2018, our nation boasted more than 32 million enterprises, of which just over 6 million had paid employees.[1] The latter equated to a business for every 55 Americans, or, better still, a business having paid employees for roughly every 30 Americans in the labor force.

Given those statistics, if one were to look at the total number of businesses, there would be a business for every five Americans in the labor force, which is astounding.

How has this been made possible?

The abundance of businesses in America owes itself to three factors: An educated workforce, a ready supply of capital, and a strong rule of law. The United States is not alone in this; in no small way, these contributors to business formation lie at the foundation of the economy of every highly developed nation.

In the Beginning Is the Idea

Most businesses start with an idea, which usually takes the form of a solution to a problem. The key question is how to build a profitable business model around the idea.

In 1995 Larry Page and Sergey Brin, who had met as graduate students at Stanford, saw that searching the internet for relevant information was a cumbersome process. Their idea was to make internet searches efficient, productive, and user-driven, applying the technology they created to drive a high level of search demand.

They didn't know how this idea could translate into a profitable business model. No one could have foreseen how dominant and profitable Google, the company they created, was to become. Certainly not Page and Brin, who in 1999 briefly entertained selling Google to Excite, a more established search engine company, for $750,000, which would have allowed them to turn a tidy profit and return to their graduate studies. No one could have blamed them for

Sergey Brin, left, and Larry Page posing in a messy office setting in October 2002
Credit: © Michael Grecco Productions, Inc./Grecco.com, ALL RIGHTS RESERVED.

unloading their money-losing venture; that year, Google had posted a $3.1 million loss on revenues of just $220,000.

Just two years later, the company would produce its first profit of $32 million on revenues of $86.4 million, and it would never look back. Three years after that, they took Google public. Between 2004 and 2019, Page and Brin sold over $10 billion of Google shares apiece, and yet still held onto corporate shares valued at more than $25 billion for each of them.

Over the next two years, the company they founded continued to prosper. By the end of 2021, with a net worth estimated by *Forbes* of $123 billion, Larry Page ranked as the fifth-richest person in the world. His former partner, Sergey Brin, was effectively tied at number six, with a reported net worth of $118.5 billion.

Unicorn Likelihood

This brings up the interesting topic of the likelihood of anyone—including you or me—becoming a billionaire. Looking to the richest among us makes an interesting study, because these subjects provide insight into the most compelling business models in each generation.

As of the end of 2020, there were over 3,200 billionaires in the world, of which over a quarter resided in the United States.[2] The odds of an American being a billionaire are roughly 1 in 355,000, or far better than the extremely long odds of winning a Powerball lottery, which is approximately 1 in 300 million.

Of course, many of the world's richest inherited their wealth, and so might be excluded from the competition to become billionaires. A better question might be this: What are the odds of being a *self-made* billionaire? Not too bad, actually; of the global population of billionaires surveyed at the end of 2020, 60% were self-made, which is an astonishing statistic.[3] The amount of wealth created in the 50 years between 1970 and 2020 is indeed almost without precedent. One would have to look to the same period a hundred years earlier for a comparative period of productivity and creativity. Instead of names like Bezos, Musk, Gates, and Buffett, one might have spoken of Rockefeller, Carnegie, and Morgan. Still, the numbers of the world's most affluent today dwarf those of the Gilded Age, or what is also called the Age of the Second Industrial Revolution.

Of course, much of the difference in the magnitude of today's superrich lies in population growth. Much is also owed to enhancements in capital formation, including resources such as the Small Business Administration, venture capital, and pervasive private equity firms. These resources, together with technological advances, gave rise to what is today called the Third Industrial Revolution, with economic and productivity growth propelled by digital and technology advances.

The numbers show that being a billionaire is statistically easier than winning the Powerball. It is also statistically easier than making a living on the PGA Tour. There were an estimated 927 billionaires in the US at the end of 2020. Meanwhile, the career earnings of the active golfer ranked 927 on the PGA Tour amounted to less than $25,000.[4] There are more self-made billionaires in America than there are PGA Tour pros who can earn a good living playing the game.

Getting into the NBA is nearly equally hard, with just 450 players scattered across 30 teams, and each earning a median salary of approximately $3.5 million in 2019.[5] Getting into the NFL is a little easier, with about 1,900 players and a far lower median salary under $850,000.[6] Yet, you would be right to say that all these people are virtual "unicorns," or mythical creatures, which is also a term used today for start-up businesses having valuations of a billion dollars and up.

Odds of Success

To my way of thinking, the real action in business lies in the middle markets, which I would characterize as companies having from $10 million to $1 billion in revenues. This is where most of the job growth and business creativity is in the United States. This is the most common fertile ground for growing businesses that have the best chances for material wealth creation.

To be among the broad group of thousands of middle market businesses is broadly attainable.

By contrast, smaller companies often serve as vehicles for independent employment, which can be personally rewarding but generally lessen the chances for wealth creation.

The bottom line is this: If you can harness an idea and transform it into a business model, what are the odds of success?

It turns out that the odds of having a business that survives at least five years are about the same as the odds of consistently breaking 100 at golf. The odds of business survival for longer than 10 years are somewhat better than regularly posting golf scores under 90.

Golf vs. Business

Golf[1]	Business[2]
50% Can't Break 100	20% Don't survive a year
25% Shoot between 90 and 100	50% Survive at least five years
20% Shoot between 80 and 90	33% Survive more than 10 years
5% Shoot below 80	?? Survive and create MVA

[1] Data from National Golf Foundation
[2] US Small Business Administration Office of Advocacy June 2016

Actually, the odds may be about the same, since golf statistics are based up players who report their scores. Of course, many golfers elect not to report their scores, while among those who do report their scores, there are well-founded suspicions of score embellishment.

In business, there are generally no free mulligans, and statistics are not compiled from self-reporting, which makes reported business survival rates more reliable.

Businesses that survive 10 or more years are apt to have better business models than those who do not. The outliers in business are the companies that do two things: They survive; and then having survived, they become worth more than they cost to create. These lie at the heart of wealth creation. The aggregate creation of value beyond the cost to create a company is called market value added

(MVA). A company's owners tend to be the prime beneficiaries of MVA, though creditors also typically benefit. The principal driver of MVA creation is centered in the ability of a business to realize rates of return that *exceed the overall cost of capital, which includes both equity and interest-costing proceeds from other people and institutions.* At an extreme level, outlier businesses can enable their shareholders to become unicorns. I expect that most of the founders of such rarified companies end up as surprised as Sergey Brin and Larry Page. But there are thousands of MVA-creating businesses that individually and collectively lie at the center of our economy and the prosperity of our communities.

The Six Variables

While there is a limitless supply of ideas that might be applicable to business formation, there is not, at a high level, a limitless supply of business models. When viewed abstractly, just Six Variables combine to deliver equity returns and create equity market value added. They are:

1. Sales
2. Business investment
3. Operating profit margin
4. Amount of interest costing proceeds (other people's money)
5. Cost of other people's money
6. Annual maintenance capital expense

This is not to say that buried within the Six Variables lie far more diverse operational fundamentals. Henry Ford created the first scalable automotive assembly line, and Albert P. Sloan was an administrative and marketing genius who grew General Motors to surpass Ford and become the largest company in the world. These and other operationally minded business leaders are illustrative of the immense creativity that can be harnessed to enhance business models. Still, behind all this effort and operational creativity lie Six Variables, which demand the attention of—and can help—every business leader.

Chapter 2
Daymond John and the First Variable

Growing up in Hollis, Queens, Daymond John was just 10 years old when he started working after-school jobs, such as handing out flyers for $2 an hour. By the time he graduated from Bayside High School, he had significant entrepreneurial experience and a strong work ethic. Juggling jobs and a desire to work for himself, he began selling t-shirts and later turned to the emerging hip-hop culture for clothing inspiration. In 1989, he began to sell headwear, and then shirts branded with his company's name, FUBU, which stands for "For Us By Us." Early on in this endeavor, Daymond's mother taught him to sew, and when he received his first big orders for $300,000 from a single Las Vegas retailer convention in 1994, he returned to their home to set up production. But he needed cash to pay for the means of production—sewing machines, fabric, employees. With orders in hand, Daymond approached banks to obtain a loan, and was declined 26 times.[1] So, he and his mother took out a $120,000 mortgage on their house to enable him to acquire the eight sewing machines and the material he needed to fulfill his orders. He also hired eight tailors. For the next two years, the home he shared with his mother would become his factory.

Daymond John (bottom left), Carl Brown, J. Alexander Martin, and Keith Perrin, the
entrepreneurs behind FUBU, pose for a photo in their New York City offices in 1999.
(Tyler Mallory/FTWP)

The money Daymond had borrowed was sufficient to fulfill his order and make a decent profit, but having done so, he was virtually broke—and new orders were coming in. He had failed to factor in the need to pay in advance for his material, which took 120 days to arrive from overseas. To add to his challenge, he had to deal with the delay in cash flow arising from the manufacturing time. The ultimate cash flow pain point was the 120-day payment terms he offered his retailers. As a result, his liquidity had to accommodate a revenue cycle that spanned more than 240 days, not to mention the growth he was experiencing from new orders. In desperation, with just $500 left in his bank account and no banks to assist him, he took out an ad in *The New York Times* that said, "A million dollars in orders. Need Financing." Fortunately, someone at Samsung Americas textile division saw and answered the advertisement, helping avert a financial disaster. Over the next 25 years, Daymond John's companies sold $6 billion in clothing, and he became a nationwide celebrity on the cast of the syndicated reality show *Shark Tank*.

Daymond John freely shares the story of his early brush with business failure. I heard the story from him when he was speaking to the Inside Track Forum, which is an event that STORE Capital annually sponsors for its customers to inspire and teach them. When looking back on his self-taught experience as an entrepreneur, Daymond wishes that he had started FUBU with a greater degree of financial literacy. His first big financial lesson, which nearly cost him his business, was this: "What Is Business Investment?" *This important question is where business model frameworks start and is the first of six universal financial variables that collectively guide investor returns.*

It is common for people to think of business investment as chiefly plant and equipment. Such a notion is also somewhat consistent with accounting terminology, where assets are divided between those that are "long-term" and those that are "short-term," or "current." When I ask students to define business investment, they think predominantly of long-term assets, such as real estate or machinery. Daymond John knew investment to be more than this. He had eight sewing machines. But then he also had to purchase the fabric and pay the eight tailors to sew his garments. In accounting terms, both these costs together would be included in inventory. So, Daymond knew he had to make inventory and equipment purchases. However, he had to tie up his cash in raw material inventory for 120 days before he took possession of it. In accounting terms, that would be a deposit. This meant that, while waiting for the fabric to arrive, he would still have to carry some operating costs. And, once the completed garments shipped, he would have to wait another 120 days to be paid. In accounting terms, that would be classified as an account receivable. So, altogether, the business investment needed to operate FUBU on an ongoing basis included five major components:

1. Sewing machines and other equipment.
2. Deposits paid by the company for the raw material inventory.
3. Inventory, which included the combined cost of the fabric and labor to produce the garments.
4. Accounts receivable.
5. Cash

The last business investment component is cash, which is needed to absorb start-up costs like general and administrative costs, utilities, and other operating costs to be borne prior to the receipt of revenues. Cash is also a good thing to have in case of unforeseen expenses or delays in the corporate cash flow cycle caused by elevated levels of inventory or delays in accounts receivable collection. All good business plans need to have margins for error, and the most important margin of error insurance is centered in liquidity access.

If, for the sake of argument, Daymond John fulfilled nothing but this one-time order for his product, then the business investment would be effectively liquidated as the deposits went away upon inventory receipt, the inventory vanished upon its sale, and the receivables likewise disappeared upon their collection. Effectively, the company would profitably liquidate as the cash flow cycle played out. However, over time, FUBU received and fulfilled many orders, and went on to achieve sales of $350 million within a decade. These investments not only recurred but grew far larger over time.

Daymond needed money to carry these five major investment components that comprised his business investment.

As FUBU grew and achieved success, the relative amount of business investment required would be expected to decrease, and the company's liquidity would increase. That is because the sellers of fabric would be less likely to require deposits from a successful and proven company. In fact, they might have offered payment terms for the fabric. Accounts payable to vendors are a reduction from business investment because they are unsecured claims on a business and often cost nothing. The vendor gives you title to the fabric in exchange for an unsecured, often free, obligation to pay at a later date.

With success would also come bankability, which would allow the company to have banks provide letters of credit that would guarantee vendor payments without tying up company cash.

Had Daymond John been able to secure his initial inventory without tying up cash for 120 days, his liquidity would have improved. Better still, if he had trade vendor terms on his inventory that would enable him to pay for the inventory long after he received it, his liquidity would have improved a lot. Had his buyers been willing to pay faster than 120 days after merchandise receipt, that would also stand to raise his liquidity.

Finally, there is often the potential for businesses to radically alter their operating model. For instance, had Daymond John been able to have the seller of the fabric also fabricate the garments, deliver them to him, wait for payment, and have his customers agree to pay faster, he would have had greatly improved liquidity, together with less invested in sewing machines and staffing.

In essence, he would have adopted an "asset light" operating model that would require even less corporate liquidity, with fixed overhead and equipment costs transformed into less risky variable expenditures. Operating model creativity entails considering such options and exploring their feasibility to improve business model efficiency that can elevate the potential for value creation.

With all these possible changes to his business model, Daymond John stood to lower his required business investment, potentially materially.

Businesses have diverse cash flow cycles. In the case of a manufacturer like FUBU, it is common to have vendor trade payables that are small relative to the inventory and accounts receivable required to operate the business. A restaurant business will be just the opposite. The cash receipts from sales are immediate. Inventory levels are low because the inventory tends to be sold every three days or so. Meanwhile, the trade payables from food vendors might come with 30-day terms, meaning that you could literally sell your inventory 10 times over before ever paying for the first inventory you had.

Accountants vs. Entrepreneurs

If you think in accounting terms, you probably think of business investment as the "left side" of a balance sheet, which is where the assets are. I do not view business investment in this light. I am a finance person, which is the foundation for accounting, but one step removed.

Finance is like music; it is a universal language, whereas accounting is not.

There exist multiple global accounting standards, which are subject to frequent changes. The dominant standards are US Generally Accepted Accounting Principles (GAAP) and International Financial Reporting Standards (IFRS), which is used by much of the rest of the world. With that said, GAAP is widely used globally among larger companies owing to its requirement for a US stock exchange listing. Accounting was devised to represent financial reality to investors and financial statement readers. However, the reflection will always have material imperfections. This is why there are so many analysts who make a living from interpreting financial statements. This is why financially inclined value investors pore over financial statements to see what the markets cannot.

From a finance perspective, total assets as they appear on a corporate financial statement do not equal business investment. To arrive at business investment, a financial analyst must ignore all the non-cash accounting conventions. This means that items like "accumulated depreciation," which is designed to illustrate the cumulative "wear and tear costs" of a business on its hard assets, need to be added back. It's not that assets don't have wear and tear; they do. It's that the wear and tear does nothing to alter what the assets originally cost. Wear and tear does not alter the business investment. Since the accounting profession has added numerous non-cash financial reporting conventions over the years, you can be busy eliminating balance sheet items.

The somewhat shameful fact is this: If you are looking at a corporate financial statement and actually trying to understand business investment, the number is nowhere reported. Our accounting profession has wrongfully determined that it is unimportant to keep track of what assets originally cost.

The next chapter will discuss the "right side" of the accounting balance sheet, which discloses liabilities and shareholder equity. But as a finance professional, some of the liabilities must be netted against cash assets at cost to arrive at business investment. Those liabilities are the ones having no cost and no claim on the assets of a business. Normally, there are two such liabilities: accounts payable and accruals. We have already briefly discussed the first of these, which represents trade vendors who are willing to give you clear title to their merchandise and then wait a period for payment. The second of these represents the timing gap between a service being provided and payment for that service. The most major example of this is employee wages; employees come to work and then generally must wait two weeks for their paycheck. There might be other unsecured, non-interest-paying cash obligations, such as customer deposits, which would be shown on the financial statement as a deferred income liability.

Variable #1: Business Investment

Number 1 of the Six Variables is business investment. To determine it, simply net accounts payable, accruals, and other unsecured, non-interest-paying cash obligations against the cash assets at cost. A short version of the business investment variable is shown below. Later on, I will expand this important variable to show its components.

Business Investment =
Cash Assets at Cost – Unsecured, Non-Interest-Paying Cash Obligations

While the accounting profession may have difficulty determining what business investment is, entrepreneurs generally can zero in on the number. One thing they know is that a lower business investment is better than a higher investment because it requires less funding. Certainly, the growth in global supply chain technology sophistication has played a role in the rise of "asset light" as a business term. If you can have less inventory, have extended trade credit terms, outsource your manufacturing, and then sell your product with fast payment terms, your required business investment can be substantially reduced. Had Daymond John been more "asset light" at the outset, his business investment requirement would have fallen materially, his liquidity would have substantially risen, and his risk of business failure reduced. As I learned a long time ago when I started out in banking, "Companies do not go out of business because they lose money. They go out of business because they run out of cash."

Chapter 3
The Capital Stack and Two More Variables

Devising how to fund your business investment typically involves multiple capital sources. Those capital sources are mostly evident from the right side (or so it's always called) of the financial statement balance sheet, which is where liabilities and shareholder equity are reported. In finance vernacular, the various sources of capital used to finance business investment are often referred to as the "capital stack." In the case of Daymond John, his capital stack was simple: He personally borrowed $120,000 on a second mortgage loan on his home and then infused that cash into his company as an equity investment. Typically, capital stacks are far more intricate.

The Right Side

I have found that most investors and entrepreneurs spend far more time focusing on the left side of the balance sheet than the right. In the case of STORE Capital, the most recent company where I served as founding chief executive officer, the left side of the balance sheet was loaded with profit-center real estate assets the company owned and leased on a long-term basis to service, retail, and manufacturing companies across the country. Most of the questions I fielded from investors and analysts stemmed from these investments.

When it comes to evaluating the right side of real estate company balance sheets, many corporate observers are simply inexperienced. For one thing, most public real estate companies have similar sorts of borrowing, with the resultant interpretation that the right side of a balance sheet is less important. However, this is far from so.

In 2005, at a predecessor public company, we conceived of a novel way to use serially issued secured debt. About three years after we embarked on this process, we sold the company to an investor group that was able to fully assume the highly flexible debt we had created. The result was that our shareholders were able to realize a compound annual rate of return approximating 19%, which would not have been possible without the flexible, assumable nature of our debt obligations. Had we simply followed the well-worn path of traditional financing options employed by most other industry participants, we and our shareholders would have missed out on this opportunity.

Borrowing sources can be instrumental in elevating shareholder rates of return, improving corporate flexibility, and even protecting shareholders in the event of severe economic turbulence.

Other People's Money (OPM)

When conceiving a corporate capital stack, there is an order of operations. At a high level, your analysis should begin with how much you *can* borrow, and then back into how much equity investment you might *need*. In the example of FUBU, Daymond John had no access to corporate borrowings when he founded the company. So, he made a $120,000 equity investment into FUBU that was funded by a personal loan he had to collateralize with his home. That small, but meaningful, investment ended up generating over $6 billion in revenues, ultimately making Daymond John an amazing financial success story. Over my years in business, I have seen similar success stories and have been proud to play a role in our customers' achievements.

As a finance professional, I do not think personally about borrowings when considering how a business should be capitalized. That is too simplistic. Instead, I think about "other people's money" (OPM). For instance, STORE Capital is in the business of owning the profit-center real estate of companies and then leasing it to them on a long-term basis. There are numerous companies that use a lot of real estate in their business (think restaurants, fitness clubs, retailers, and many more) and they have a problem to solve. They could own the real estate and seek bank financing, or they could instead lease the real estate from a company like STORE.

Real estate ownership requires an equity investment that can typically range as high as 40%, paired with borrowings for the remaining 60% plus. The alternative is to have a company like STORE put up all the money for the real estate, buy it, and then lease it back to you on a long-term lease. The amount of OPM entailed is different. A real estate lease offers far more OPM than does the choice of real estate ownership. Yet both are viable choices when it comes to creating a corporate capital stack.

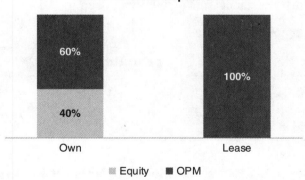

Lease vs. Own Capital Stacks

As a self-described "finance guy," I could care less about the accounting treatment of my capital stack. My attention tends to turn in the direction of equity returns, corporate flexibility, liquidity, and margins for error, which are important keys to value and wealth creation. I find that most corporate CEOs feel likewise. Hence, some will choose to own equipment or real estate, while others will elect to lease equipment and real estate. Either way, these decisions impact the corporate OPM and equity mix. They impact the capital stack.

Accountants like to include within company liabilities non-interest-costing obligations, such as trade payables, deposits (deferred income), and accrued liabilities. As a finance guy, I ignore such liabilities within the corporate capital stack. Since they cost nothing to me, I subtract them from the amount I would otherwise have to make to determine business investment, the first of the Six Variables, which was discussed in the preceding chapter.

Borrowings at cost are generally visible on a corporate financial statement, while the cost of leased assets is nowhere to be seen. Accountants have always been obsessed with lease accounting, which embodies why accounting is always going to be an imperfect reflection of financial reality. For most of my career, real estate leases were not included on a balance sheet at all. They just showed up in the form of rent expense, and required a detailed financial statement footnote disclosure explaining how much in lease payments the company was obligated to pay over time. All of this changed with new accounting rules imposed in 2019.

GAAP Lease Accounting

	Old Rules	2019 Rules
Show an Asset?	No	Yes
Show a Liability?	No	Yes
Show OPM Proceeds?	No	No

In 2019, new lease accounting standards set by the Financial Accounting Standards Board (FASB) were enacted, resulting in the creation of non-cash "right to use" assets and liabilities, representing the estimated present values of lease payment obligations.[1] Since a lease is generally not a debt substitute, but instead a debt and equity substitute, the amount of the "right to use" liability and asset created will typically not approximate the actual amount of the OPM represented by your decision to lease.

Variables #2 and #3: Amount and Cost of OPM

A company's capital stack provides numbers two and three of the Six Variables at the hands of corporate leadership to deliver investor returns.

- The second of the Six Variables is the OPM/equity mix.
- The third variable is the cost of OPM.

In starting a company, business owners understand fully the cost of assets they choose to rent instead of buy. Business owners also understand the amount of money they borrow from banks and other sources. Add the two together and you get the second variable, the amount of OPM used in a business.

OPM =
Borrowings at Cost + Assets You Elected to Lease, Rather than Buy, at Cost

In determining current investor returns, the cost of OPM is paired with the amount of OPM used to arrive at the third equation variable. The simple formula is as follows:

Cost of OPM =
(Interest Paid on Borrowings + Rents on Assets That Could Have Been Owned)

÷

(Amount of Borrowings + Cost of Lease Proceeds Deployed)

If you were computing the cost of OPM for a year, you would take the total amount of interest and lease payments shown above and then divide them into the average of the loan principal outstanding and the cost of the leased assets deployed. When it comes to determining the cost of OPM, my treatment of leases can seem simplistic, because leases often have escalators built into them and sometimes allow for an accumulation of equity with a future known purchase option. But, as you will see as we go on, I am most interested in computing a current investor rate of return, and not a theoretical total rate of return. To do this requires that I simply compute a current cost of OPM.

Cost of Capital vs. Cost of Equity

A corporate capital stack is comprised solely of interest-costing OPM, together with equity that is likewise demanding of a return. If you can take the total annual OPM interest and lease cost, together with the desired current annual rate of return for equity investors, and then divide that cost by the amount of your capital stack, you can determine your current annual corporate cost of capital. Then, if you can realize current corporate returns that exceed that cost of capital, you have market value added (MVA), creating a business worth more than its cost. The whole is now worth more than the sum of the cost of its parts.

In golfing terms, you have broken par, which is a feat few can accomplish.

Corporate cost of capital is a frequent topic of conversation in business schools. However, I decided some time ago that the only thing that really mattered from a mathematical point of view was the cost of equity. After all, entrepreneurs are not trying to make their lenders, equipment owners, or landlords rich. They are trying to make their *equity* owners rich.

So, to keep it simple, the important metric to know is not corporate market value added. It's equity market value added, which is the amount by which the value of corporate equity exceeds its historic cost.

When it comes to your capital stack, you want to strike a balance between OPM and equity having the potential to deliver the highest equity rate of return. Hence, in the order of operations to determining a capital stack, you start with the amount of OPM you can attain and then back into the amount of equity you require. When it comes to equity, less tends to be more.

Capital Stack Assembly

During my business career, I gained something of a reputation for creating financial models. Not to be outdone, Mort Fleischer—my mentor and business partner for most of those years—created "Mort's Model," which he had framed, and then freely passed around, and which I will immortalize here. Mort's Model embodies the notion of less equity is more, and goes like this:

Mort's Model

Operating Cash Flow ÷ Yenem's Gelt = ∞

"Yenem's Gelt" is Yiddish for OPM, and "∞," otherwise called a "lazy eight," is the mathematical notation for infinity, which is supposed to be the resultant equity return. The formula is intended to convey that a business generating cash flow and funded entirely with OPM will yield an infinite rate of return to the owners of the business. Of course, equity rates of return would not be computed this way. Instead, operating cash flow would be divided into the equity investment of zero to arrive at an effective infinite rate of return. Mort simply wanted to make the point of the importance of OPM. Saying it in Yiddish elevated the amusement level. In my years in business, I have seen a number of people successfully start or buy businesses with no equity. It is possible, but not easy.

Consistent with Mort's Model, forming a capital stack begins with a determination of the maximum amount of OPM you can get. In the end, you may not want to maximize your use of OPM, but it is good to know the art of the possible. As I noted in the conclusion to the last chapter, companies go out of business because they run out of cash. So, understanding where liquidity can be accessed outside of business operating cash flow is important. Plus, understanding how to maximize OPM will give you the best shot of minimizing equity and achieve something close to Mort's Model.

Corporate Capital Stack =
OPM + Equity

At a high level, when it comes to the puzzle of how to assemble an equity stack, there are just three simple steps:

Step 1: Start with money that has the longest repayment requirements. Hard assets like real estate and equipment can be financed for a long time and may even be leased.

Another area where long-term money is to be found is with asset-based loans (ABLs), whereby lenders advance money against accounts receivable and inventory. Such loans are often in the form of lines of credit that can mature in a year or two. However, they require no repayment and can generally be readily extended, since they are based on accepted formulaic advance rates against assets that can be easily valued. Accountants often think of such credit lines as short-term, owing to their debt maturity time frame. Finance experts tend to think differently, because they know such lines to be readily extendable.

Another source of long-term money, if you are buying a business, can be in the form of notes payable to the prior owner, which are often unsecured corporate obligations.

Financing assets through OPM that involve long-term repayment (as in equipment or real estate loans) or modest to no repayment (as in equipment leases, real estate leases, or ABL facilities) provides several benefits: OPM can be maximized, monthly payments can be minimized, and the capital stack can be stable.

OPM that is repaid quickly will alter the capital stack over time to elevate equity. That may sound nice, but an altered capital stack will tend to lower equity returns and potentially lessen corporate cash flow that can otherwise be invested in expansion. Repaying OPM and tilting the capital stack to 100% equity is fine, so long as your business has nothing more productive to do with the cash.

Step 2: Your next step is to turn to short-term money. In general, this will be money that has limited collateral and is repayable from free cash flows expected to be thrown off by the business after all the other OPM obligations have been met. Such loans will tend to amortize more quickly and represent a more volatile form of OPM because they are less universally available. Economic cycles come and go, lender risk tolerance rises and falls, and corporate cash flow loans are the most vulnerable to such changing environments.

There may be an order of operations to determining OPM and a capital stack, but there is no standard OPM portion of a capital stack. Daymond John was declined 26 times for bank loans before finally borrowing money from a subsidiary of a South Korean conglomerate that he would not have found but for his newspaper advertisement. Indeed, commercial banks are not all the same. Likewise, there are a myriad of equipment and real estate leasing companies having diverse views of investment risk. And then there are non-bank lenders, such as small business investment companies (SBICs), business development companies (BDCs), and a host of non-bank direct lenders that collectively amounted to over $800 billion in assets at the end of 2019 from less than $30 billion in deployed capital in 2000.

When it comes to OPM, there is a lot to choose from, which means that it's important to be informed and selective. Take time to shop.

Step 3: Your final step is to determine the amount of equity required. Once the OPM portion of the capital stack is determined, then the amount of equity you require is simple. It's the difference between your required business investment and OPM.

$$\text{Equity} =$$
$$\text{Business Investment} - \text{OPM}$$

Equity Sourcing

Having solved for the required amount of equity, the question is, where does the equity come from? In the case of Daymond John, he was unable to get any OPM to start up FUBU, so he had to put up all the money himself in the form of equity by pledging a personal asset to the bank. He would later get OPM from Samsung and others as he grew FUBU into the success that it became.

As you might guess from our discussions up to now, there is a limit to the amount of equity you should invest. Equity is entitled to all the free cash flow remaining after paying the OPM obligations. The relationship of that free cash flow to the equity you invest, combined with the potential growth of that cash flow and the risks in the business, will determine whether you have the potential to create EMVA.

Equity does not have to all come from you. Most entrepreneurs I have known began their careers with little in the way of financial resources. After he became a financial success story, Daymond John landed a spot as a "shark" on the syndicated show *Shark Tank*. Each week, select entrepreneurs seeking capital to start or grow their business would pitch their offerings to Daymond and other sharks, all highly successful businesspeople, in the hopes of raising added equity without giving away too much of their companies. In essence, the sharks became OPM equity for business founders and brought with them added skills to help the companies (and their personal investments) succeed. With that said, for simplicity I will start with the notion that all equity is your own money, which I also call YOM. OPM equity will be a subject for later.

Chapter 4

Three More Variables and Voilà!

Businesses have nearly infinite operational possibilities. A company always starts with an idea that can be sold, such as an internet search engine algorithm or a clothing line. Then that idea or business model must first be expressed in terms of an income statement. What are the start-up costs? What is the cost to produce and deliver the product? How will the product be priced? How much will the corporate overhead be? If your business requires real estate or equipment, how much money will be required every year to maintain or replace assets used in the business?

Operational questions pertaining to business investment are no less numerous. How will your product be made? How much real estate and equipment do you need to make the product? Can you outsource any of the product manufacturing? What are your inventory needs? Do you have to provide deposits against inventory orders? Can you get terms from your trade vendors? How fast will your customers pay you? Can you get customer deposits?

In all business models, there is a cycle of interdependence. Operational fundamentals reflected in your income statement are key to the determination of your business investment and OPM, which comprise the first three universal business model variables. In turn, your business investment and OPM are impacted by the income statement, which is the source of the final three universal business model variables.

We have already discussed the three variables pertaining to business investment and the amount and cost of OPM. This leaves the remining three important variables that are associated with the income statement.

Variable #4: Sales

Sales is where every business starts. Sales is principally a function of customer count, product price, and average purchases per customer. For the purposes of our analysis, sales are shown on an accounting basis, meaning that they are accrued and not cash sales. In many financial models I have seen, companies do what is called a *cash budget*, and so only show sales happening when the cash is received. Here, thinking of the discussion in chapter 2, Daymond John's first sales order was for $300,000, and so the sales would be shown as soon as the garments were delivered to the customer, even though the cash from the sales would not be received until four months later.

In my approach, using a cash budget approach is unnecessary, which means that accrual-based, accountant-prepared numbers are just fine to use. The fact that the cash from sales may not be immediately collected is already taken into consideration by virtue of the definition of business investment, which includes the cash flow lag represented by accounts receivable as an investment.

Variable #5: Operating Profit Margin

This is the amount of earnings before interest, taxes, depreciation (and other non-cash accounting conventions), together with the rent expense you have on assets you could otherwise have elected to purchase (EBITDAR) shown as a percentage of revenues. When it comes to rents, you might have to lease office space or storefront space in a multi-tenanted building, which you would never have otherwise purchased. That type of rent is simply an annual expense. Then there is the rent on free-standing buildings or aircraft or machinery that you could have otherwise purchased. The proceeds from lease providers used to purchase these assets are a part of OPM and so this expense is backed out of operating expense to compute EBITDAR. Depreciation is an accounting non-cash convention designed to mimic a charge for wear and tear use of building and equipment you own and, like all non-cash accounting numbers in our definitions, is excluded. As with sales above, expenses can be derived from accountant prepared financial statements, even though the expenses may not all be in cash. That is because accrued expenses and trade payables are embodied as a deduction in the definition of business investment. With that said, computing an operating profit margin is simple:

$$\textbf{Operating Profit Margin} = \text{EBITDAR} \div \text{Sales}$$

It is important that company expenses include market compensation to be paid to the leadership group. When leaders are the founders or shareholders of a company, they often exclude their own compensation when creating a business model, simply thinking that they will be paid from corporate profits. In doing so, they miss an important point: If they were not there, they would have to hire someone else to run the company. The idea is that the operating profit margin should be there to cover the cost of OPM, the cost of annual maintenance capital expense (the discussion for this cost follows), and the returns to equity investors. You should never mistake market-based employee compensation for your equity return.

Variable #6: Annual Maintenance Capital Expense

Also called "maintenance capex," the final income statement variable is actually not an accounting income statement expense at all. The presence of this variable is another example of where finance and accounting diverge. Accountants use depreciation as a proxy for maintenance capex, but, since it is a convention, the number will be wrong.

STORE Capital is a poster child for how depreciation conventions deviate from reality. Annually, STORE records significant amounts of depreciation expenses on the real estate it holds. Yet, over the company's history, real estate sold has realized aggregate prices that have exceeded its cost. In other words, the real estate did not depreciate in value at all, which is why investors customarily ignore this expense when looking at the financial performance of many real estate-centric businesses. Real estate is far from alone with depreciation conventions that can part ways with reality. Businesses owning assets ranging from heavy construction equipment to aircraft often have income statements loaded with depreciation expenses that exceed actual costs associated with wear and tear.

Since every accounting entry has an opposing entry, the opposing entry to depreciation expense is a corresponding reduction in asset cost. As with the frequent errors associated with wear-and-tear estimation, this is also wrong, because the prices of hard asset investments never change unless you sell them or add on to them. Non-cash accounting conventions like depreciation simply do not reflect financial reality, which is why I exclude them.

If you have a business that requires the use of real estate or equipment, you will absolutely have annual costs to maintain or replace the assets, and you should estimate the annual amount of these future costs. Chances are that, in earlier years, maintenance capex will be low, since new equipment or real estate requires less upkeep. Later on, the maintenance costs can be expected to rise. For example, if you operate a consumer-facing business, you may want to remodel your storefront every five years to have a fresher look. From a financial point of view, such costs should be averaged and included as an annual corporate expense. I cannot tell you how many times I have seen companies expend huge amounts on remodeled storefronts and call this a "non-recurring" expense. That is often a means for business leaders to exclude certain costs to make their near-term operating results look better than they really are.

Putting the Six Variables Together

With the Six Variables defined, it is time to illustrate how a company works. To make things simple I chose a restaurant. The first company I helped take public in 1994 was initially exclusively devoted to financing restaurant real estate, and restaurants tended to have comparatively simple business models. Here is the illustrative model that we will use throughout this book:

Restaurant Case Study

1 Business Investment		$1,000,000
2 Sales		1,500,000
3 Operating Profit (EBITDAR)	Profit margin is 20% of revenues	300,000
4 Maintenance CapEx	2% of business investment annually	20,000
5 OPM	OPM is 75% of business investment	750,000
6 Interest and Rent Expense	Cost of OPM is 9%	67,500
7 Pre-Tax Cash Flow	3 - 4 - 6	212,500
8 After-Tax Cash Flow	75% of cash flow	159,375
9 Equity	Opposite of OPM (25% of business investment)	250,000
Return on Equity		
Pre-Tax	7 ÷ 9	85.0%
After-Tax	8 ÷ 9	63.8%

The model is designed to compute the current corporate return on equity, which is the foundation for wealth creation. I placed in bold the Six Variables comprising the model. Actually, there is a seventh variable, which is the income tax rate, which I assumed to be 25%. Therefore, the after-tax cash flow on line 8 is 75% of the pre-tax cash flow. As we move forward, I will often ignore taxes because the taxes from the earnings of most companies in America are passed through to their shareholders.

Our restaurant cost $1 million in business investment, does $1.5 million in sales annually, has an EBITDAR profit margin of 20% of sales, spends 2% of its original business investment annually in maintenance capex, has annual interest and rent expense (OPM cost) of $67,500, and delivers $212,500 to its shareholders. To fund the business investment, the shareholders were able to borrow or lease 75% of the money at an annual cost of 9%. Comparing the restaurant's pre-tax cash flow to the YOM equity investment of $250,000 results in a current pre-tax return on equity of 85%. The current after-tax rate of return is 63.75%.

You are potentially thinking that an 85% annual pre-tax rate of return sounds too good to be true. The average return on stock and bond investments is a fraction of this. In fact, the returns from an investment in Berkshire Hathaway (which became a STORE shareholder), led by legendary investor Warren Buffett, approximated 20% from 1965 through 2020. I would note that Berkshire Hathaway is a taxable corporation and so might be compared to the after-tax corporate rate of return here of 63.75%. In my experience, however, such high rates of annual return are not uncommon.

There are three important items of note.

First, this sample model is for a single restaurant and so has far more risk than a large and highly diversified company like Berkshire Hathaway.

Second, the model excludes debt principal repayment, which will lessen the cash current ROE slightly because the total OPM payment is typically higher than just the interest cost.

Finally, the return on equity is just a current rate of return. The Six Variables can and do change from year to year, sometimes a lot. You can easily guess where the real variability lies: The three largest numbers of business investment, sales, and operating profit margin. These tend to be the principal drivers of future growth as well as performance volatility. The remaining three variables are comparatively less significant and less variable.

Assuming you have shopped hard to understand your OPM alternatives, changing the OPM and equity mix can be a challenge. Same with the OPM interest cost. More than this, OPM interest cost and maintenance capex tend to be smaller numbers, which means that changes in these variables will be less impactful on equity returns.

The truth is that successful businesspeople create impressive business models capable of generating gargantuan rates of return on their initial equity investments all the time. Think of any self-made billionaire in the Forbes 400, and their historic cost basis in the equity of their company is likely small. Sergey Brin and Larry Page were doctoral students when they conceived Google, and Daymond John was working out of his home. Basically, the small relative investments they collectively made in companies that became highly successful allowed their equity returns to approach Mort's Model and be almost too high to count.

Another important characteristic of the self-made members of the Forbes 400 is that the companies they founded were highly scalable. This stands in contrast to our restaurant. Restaurants tend to have little operating leverage, which is the ability to grow revenues with minimal added business investment. For our restaurant operator to materially grow revenues, new restaurants will have to be built, requiring a corresponding increase in business investment. As a result, there were just six members of the 2021 Forbes 400 list of wealthiest Americans whose net worth was centered in restaurant operations. Of these fortunate few, five benefited not simply from food service operations, but from other activities, such as product sales, franchising, and real estate rental revenues, as well. Generally speaking, restaurant business models are simply not good enough to earn inclusion into this elite status.

As noted earlier, business model variables can and do move around. Sales and operating profit margins can change. The capital stack can also change. For instance, we are starting out with a company using 75% of OPM and 25% of equity. However, if you repay the OPM, then the mix of equity will correspondingly move up, which will lower the current equity rates of return. Then there is revenue, which can be subject to constant change. If sales were to rise by 5%, then the current pre-tax return on equity would rise to 91%. With another sales increase of 5%, the current pre-tax equity return would rise another 6% or so to 97%. While it's common for business professionals to evaluate investment opportunities using multiyear models, business model variables can and do change frequently from year to year in ways that can materially alter current equity returns.

Gordon Growth Model

If our simple restaurant financial model shows just the current annual rate of return, what might be the *total* rate of return? A common way to think of this is to use a variant of what is called the Gordon Growth Model, which simply adds a constant growth rate to a current rate of return, to arrive at a total expected rate of return. Taking our initial model, let's assume that sales increase 5% annually, resulting in a long-term equity return growth rate approximating 6%. To estimate total expected pre-tax equity rates of return, all you need to do is to add the 6% in annual return growth to the beginning 85% current pre-tax equity return to achieve an estimated total pre-tax equity rate of return of 91%.

Gordon Growth Model
Expected Yield + Constant Growth Rate = Total Rate of Return

In the case of our restaurant illustration, the current equity rate of return is high, while the expected annual rate of sales growth is expected to result in a low rate of return growth over time. On the other hand, most highly valued growth companies tend to have lower current rates of equity return, combined with materially higher expected annual growth rates.

The Gordon Growth model, also called the Gordon Equation, was devised by American economist Myron Gordon in 1956 while an associate professor at MIT and is widely used in the investment community. For example, through the end of 2019, our five-year average dividend yield at STORE Capital approximated 4.5%. Add that to the annual growth rate of our adjusted funds from operations per share (AFFO, which is intended to approximate a stabilized equity cash flow growth rate), which grew at a compound rate just over

Myron Gordon at the University of Toronto in 1982
Credit: Jennifer Bremner/Joseph L. Rotman School of Management

7% annually, and you arrive at an expected average annual rate of return of better than 11%. For the five-year period from 2015 to 2019, our business model was reflected in our annual rates of return.

With publicly traded companies, business model performance does not always result in near-term equivalent investor return performance. The public markets have a way of altering relative share values due to constantly shifting investor sentiments. As public company business leaders, there is little we can do about this. What we can do is to keep our eyes on our business model with the expectation that this will ultimately be reflected in our investor return delivery.

Equity Valuation

We are now at a key moment with a final question to be answered. After all your work to create your first successful restaurant location, what is the value of your business and how much wealth have you created? As I noted very early on, the notion of wealth creation is central to the formation of financially successful companies. Companies capable of generating equity returns that create equity market value added (EMVA) are the companies that can attract outside independent investor capital to help them fulfill their growth potential. In this case, the initial equity investment was $250,000, the current pre-tax equity rate of return is 85%, with a current equity return growth rate of 6% annually. Assume that the investment community would generally be acceptable with a current annual pre-tax rate of return of 20%, given the risk of your restaurant and its prospects for growth. In that case, you now have a company having an equity valuation multiple of 4.25X more than it cost as follows:

Equity Valuation Multiple Formula

Your Current Pre-Tax Equity Rate of Return

$\div$

Required Investor Current Pre-Tax Equity Return

or

$$85\% \div 20\% = 4.25X$$

Your restaurant now has an equity value of $1,062,500, computed by taking your $250,000 equity investment and multiplying it by 4.25. After you have recovered your $250,000, the amount of wealth you have created is $812,500 ($1,062,500 − $250,000). That $812,500 is also your equity market value added, which is the value of your equity investment in excess of its creation cost.

Personally, I find it exciting that material wealth like this can often be created over a comparatively brief period, in this case by having a single successful restaurant location. What is more exciting is that this is simply where business wealth creation begins.

The Miracle of Compounding

Computing a total estimated pre-tax return of 91% by adding the current annual equity return achieved by the restaurant investment to its expected return growth rate is neat but is just the tip of the iceberg of the company's wealth creation potential.

Successful companies capitalize on potent business models by reinvesting their free cash flows. In the case of the restaurant illustration, the after-tax cash flow available to reinvest after the initial year amounts to $159,375. What if this money could be reinvested into expansion at a similar 85% current pre-tax rate of return? And what if the current pre-tax rate of return of the reinvested free cash flows, like the returns on the initial invested equity, could be expected to rise 6% annually? And what if you could achieve similar results with subsequent future free cash flows over the first five years of your business? You have now altered the nature of your initial equity investment. That investment has been transformed from a single stand-alone enterprise to one benefiting from the availability of future recurring equity investments enabled by its growing after-tax free cash flows. By reinvesting your equity cash flows, you are compounding your current investment returns.

Here's how founding father and successful entrepreneur Ben Franklin described compound returns: "Money makes money. And the money that money makes, makes money."

Leading physicist and Nobel laureate Albert Einstein reportedly once referred to compound interest as mankind's greatest invention.

Noted investor Warren Buffett frequently discussed the power of compound interest, famously noting, "My wealth has come from a combination of living in America, some lucky genes, and compound interest."

The result of this compounding is that after tax annual cash flows could be expected to rise more than 70% annually, substantially more than the growth arising from 5% annual sales increases at a single restaurant location. In taking your initial equity investment of $250,000 and then reinvesting all your company's free after-tax cash flows, you end up having nearly $3.3 million in equity at cost at the conclusion of the fifth year, including the $1.3 million in fifth year after-tax cash flows that would be reinvested in continued growth the following year. The 5% sales increases realized each year enable the growth in current after-tax returns to reach nearly 70% by the fifth year, with the resultant equity valuation multiple rising to 4.65X. Best of all, your equity is now valued at better than $9 million, of which over $7 million (the $9 million company value less the $1.9 million equity cost) is EMVA. Equity value and equity at cost are each actually $1.35 million more if one were to include the cash flows from the fifth year that have yet to be reinvested in future growth.

Your $250,000 initial equity investment made money and reinvesting the money made by your initial equity investment made even more money.

From a single equity investment offering a solid return, but modest potential for growth, emerges a larger, more diversified business having far greater growth potential driven by the benefits of return compounding. As impressive as the results are, they can get even better. The current pre-tax equity return investor hurdle rate of 20% could be expected to drop materially with the company's radically elevated growth, size, and diversity. Cutting the hurdle rate as a result of the material added growth would stand to add to EMVA, potentially significantly.

Five-Year Company Model with No Dividend Payout

($000's)	Year 1	Year 2	Year 3	Year 4	Year 5
Beginning Equity at Cost	$250	$409	$682	$1,146	$1,940
Ending Equity at Cost	$409	$682	$1,146	$1,940	$3,293
Current Reinvested After-Tax Cash Flows	$159	$272	$465	$793	$1,354
Growth Rate		*71%*	*71%*	*71%*	*71%*
Current After-Tax Return	63.75%	66.50%	68.19%	69.19%	69.79%
Equity Valuation Multiple	4.25X	4.43X	4.55X	4.61X	4.65X
Total Equity Valuation	**$1,063**	**$1,815**	**$3,098**	**$5,288**	**$9,024**

Dissecting Investment Returns

Investment returns are not hard to understand. They are generally only determined by three components: the initial amount invested, cash flows received and the change in investment value upon ultimate sale. In the case of the compounding illustration described earlier, the initial equity investment is $250,000, with the business paying no distributions, instead reinvesting the free cash flow into company growth. At the end of the fifth year, with the equity investment valued at over $9 million, the after-tax rate of return would amount to nearly 100% annually. That return is comprised of average current after tax rates of return approximating 67.5%, together with a change in value arising from the 4.65X equity valuation multiple at the conclusion of the fifth year. Of this return, approximately two thirds is derived from annual cash flows, with the remainder coming from the increase in equity valuation. Had the current pre-tax equity investor return hurdle rate fallen in half to 10%, the annual return would rise to 125%, propelled by a change in ending company value, which would deliver nearly half the expected rate of return.

(For the purpose of this return computation, I excluded $1.35 million in ending equity arising from the fifth-year free cash flow, which is sitting in the bank and awaiting deployment at the beginning of year six. I omitted the cash amount because valuing the company as a going concern implies cash flow reinvestment, which is essential to the high annual free cash flow growth rate. So, to the extent investors will pay up for growth as reflected in equity valuation multiples, the balance sheet cash is effectively already incorporated into the company's valuation.)

I like to understand where investment returns come from. Expected returns having strong contributions from current equity cash flows are less dependent on future equity valuation multiples, and are therefore less risky.

What would happen to equity returns if half of the annual after-tax free cash flows were paid out as dividends? First, the company would wind up having an ultimate equity valuation nearly 60% less than where it would have been with all its free cash flow reinvested in future growth. Annual free cash flow growth would likewise decline from 71% to 39%.

Five-Year Company Model with a 50% Dividend Payout

($000's)	Year 1	Year 2	Year 3	Year 4	Year 5
Beginning Equity at Cost	$250	$330	$440	$594	$807
Ending Equity at Cost	$330	$440	$594	$807	$1,103
Current Reinvested After-Tax Cash Flows	$80	$111	$154	$213	$296
Growth Rate		*39%*	*39%*	*39%*	*39%*
Current After-Tax Return	63.75%	67.16%	69.80%	71.80%	73.28%
Equity Valuation Multiple	4.25X	4.48X	4.65X	4.79X	4.89X
Total Equity Valuation	**$1,063**	**$1,476**	**$2,049**	**$2,844**	**$3,944**

When it comes to the expected rate of investment return, the loss of compounding by distributing half the annual free cash flow would lower the after-tax rate of return from 98% to 91%. With an ability to only reinvest half of the free cash flows into growth, I tend to prefer using what is called a modified internal rate of return computation, which assumes that the reinvestment rate of the distributed cash flows is going to be different from the return produced by the investment. In this case, if one were to assume that the reinvestment rate falls to 10%, which would be closer to the long-run return posted by the S&P 500, the return falls to 77%, with current cash flows (including those distributed) comprising approximately 90% of this amount.

IRR for a Five-Year Company Model with a 50% Dividend Payout

	Year					
	0	**1**	**2**	**3**	**4**	**5**
Initial Investment	(250)					
Dividends		80	111	154	213	296
Residual Value, Net of Tax						3,308
Total	($250)	$80	$111	$154	$213	$3,604
After Tax IRR	**91%**					
Modified IRR	**77%**					

Business model fundamentals and growth prospects vary widely, which can greatly alter return dynamics. In our restaurant illustration, the expected 5% unit-level revenue growth is modest, which is typical of a mature industry. Business models that address newer industries and large markets offering elevated growth potential will look far different. Making two simple changes to the operating margin and growth assumptions in our business model provides an illustration:

Model with 15% Operating Margin and 35% Growth

($000's)	Year 1	Year 2	Year 3	Year 4	Year 5
Beginning Equity at Cost	$250	$353	$558	$951	$1,696
Ending Equity at Cost	$353	$558	$951	$1,696	$3,095
Current Reinvested After-Tax Cash Flows	$103	$205	$393	$744	$1,399
Growth Rate		*99%*	*92%*	*89%*	*88%*
Current After-Tax Return	41.25%	57.98%	70.50%	78.26%	82.53%
Equity Valuation Multiple	2.75X	3.87X	4.7X	5.22X	5.5X
Total Equity Valuation	**$688**	**$1,365**	**$2,622**	**$4,963**	**$9,329**

With no dividends paid, the return result from compounding approximates that of our initial example. The relative return contributions of cash flows and ultimate value change is also similar. What is different is the rate of cash flow and current after-tax equity return growth. Relying on such growth imposes greater risk that the ultimate expected rate of return will be attained.

Given the power of reinvested free cash flows to elevate returns, most rapidly growing companies having potent business models choose to limit dividend distributions or share repurchases. Taking money out of such companies simply imposes performance drags.

Founding a business blessed with a solid business model capable of EMVA creation and then turbocharging EMVA growth through return compounding is among the most assured and fastest means to create material wealth that I know of, and follows a well-worn path forged by the wealthiest among us.

Chapter 5
The Value Equation

A ny business model that can be done on a brief spreadsheet, such as our restaurant model in the previous chapter, can be done shorthand. In 1999 I developed the Value Equation, or V-Formula, a tool that incorporates the Six Variables into a shortcut designed to compute corporate pre-tax current equity returns (ROE) as follows:[1]

The V-Formula

(Sales ÷ Business Investment × Operating Profit Margin
− % of OPM × Interest Rate − Annual
Maintenance CapEx ÷ Business Investment) = *Current Pre-Tax ROE*
÷
% of Equity

Now, here is the V-Formula applied to the restaurant business case study from the prior chapter:

The Case Study V-Formula

$(\$1,500,000 \div \$1,000,000 \times 20\% - 75\% \times 9\% - \$20,000 \div \$1,000,000) \div 25\%$

or

$(\$1,500,000 \div \$1,000,000 \times .2 - .75 \times .09 - \$20,000 \div \$1,000,000) \div .25$

$= .85 \text{ or } 85\%$

EVA and EMVA

The idea for creating a value equation came from my appreciation for the concept of economic value added (EVA), which was developed by consulting firm Stern Stewart & Co. and detailed by G. Bennett Stewart in his 1991 book *The Quest for Value*. The basic idea behind EVA was to take a financial approach to a corporate income statement, much as we did in the previous chapter. However, when computing EVA, you would not simply have a cost of OPM, but would also have an equity charge for the expected cost of equity. Then, to the extent you still had a profit from operations, that profit would be the amount by which your results from business operations exceeded your cost of capital (OPM and equity). The result is EVA. Over time, EVA accumulation translates into market value added (MVA), which is the amount a company is worth in excess of its cost to create. Unsurprisingly, the notions of EVA and MVA have garnered the attention of shareholder representation groups as a leading metric for corporate capital efficiency.

The primary beneficiaries of EVA creation are the equity investors in a company. Part of EVA creation may also go to OPM providers. However, if you compute your cost of OPM and discover that it exceeds the cost of OPM were you to get it today, who cares? Your OPM providers will have made a little money by having loans or leases worth more than they cost, which is fine.

I decided that trying to exceed my estimated current cost of capital was far less important than trying to exceed my current cost of equity. I also wanted a relative, easy-to-calculate metric, rather than an absolute hard number like EVA. I wanted to know my current pre-tax rate of return on equity and conceived the V-Formula to do just that. More than this, *I wanted a metric that focused only on equity value creation*, which was the inspiration for the formula. By understanding my current pre-tax equity return (in the case of our restaurant, 85%) and the return requirements investors might demand of a company having similar risks and growth prospects (in our case study, 20%), then I could calculate the equity market value added (EMVA) as follows:

Equity Market Value Added (EMVA) Computation

Current Equity Rate of Return

$\div$

Required Investor Equity Return

or

$85\% \div 20\% = 4.25X$ (Equity Valuation Multiple)

then

(Equity Valuation Multiple -1) $\times$ Equity Investment

or

$3.25 \times \$250,000$

$= \$812,500$ (EMVA)

There are two more reasons why current equity returns and EMVA are more important to know than the overall cost of capital and EVA.

First, the two V-Formula variables associated with OPM (the percent of the company funded with OPM and the cost of the OPM) are less important variables. They are not part of the Big Three variables (sales, business investment, and operating profit margin) that collectively and individually have the greatest impact on equity returns.

Second, assuming highly informed business leadership, the degree of OPM's impact on equity rates of return tends to be range-bound. OPM providers are not all the same, but the differences they make on overall corporate capital stack composition tend to be limited, assuming business leaders well-versed in OPM alternatives.

Making the V-Formula Even Simpler

As you will see throughout this book, the framework created by the V-Formula is powerful. Within just the Six Variables lie all the financial levers at the hands of business leaders that impact corporate equity returns and shareholder wealth creation.

As simple as the V-Formula is, you can make it even easier. In the case of your restaurant, the relationship represented by the first two formula variables, sales ÷ business investment, can simply be represented by a ratio of 1.5 ($1,500,000 ÷ $1,000,000). This is a key measure of business efficiency. In your case, your restaurant gets $1.50 in sales for every $1.00 invested in the business. What if you could reduce your required business investment without impacting your sales so that the ratio of sales to business investment increases to 2:1? Your current pre-tax rate of return on equity would rise to 125%, as follows:

The Case Study V-Formula
(2:1 Sales to Business Investment Ratio)

$(2 \times 20\% - 75\% \times 9\% - \$20,000 \div \$1,000,000) \div 25\% = 125\%$

Likewise, I tend to think of annual maintenance capex requirements as a percentage of business investment, which is how the variable was introduced in the prior chapter. With your restaurant, a \$20,000 annual maintenance capex cost is 2% of the \$1 million in business investment. So just use that. If the maintenance capex requirement were to change to 4%, your current pre-tax equity returns would fall a bit, to 117%.

The Case Study V-Formula
(4% Maintenance CapEx Ratio)

$$(2 \times 20\% - 75\% \times 9\% - 4\%) \div 25\% = 117\%$$

A lesson to be taken away from the above illustrations is that no numeric inputs are required to understand the ability of a corporate business model to produce current equity returns.

The potency of the V-Formula is centered in *relative* numeric relationships, such as the relationship between sales and business investment, or the relationship between maintenance capex and business investment. In terms of your capital stack, you are looking at the relationships between the percentage of the business investment funded with OPM and then between the portion of the business investment funded by OPM and the current cost of that OPM.

With the V-Formula reduced to simple relative numeric relationships, the same can be done with EMVA creation. Assuming the same investor current pre-tax return hurdle rate of 20%, then the equity valuation multiple rises from 4.25X from the initial 85% pre-tax rate of return to 5.85X at a current pre-tax rate of return of 117%. Of this amount, 4.85X (the equity valuation multiple minus 1) is EMVA creation, or just shy of 83% of your equity value. As a measurement of wealth creation efficiency, creating 4.85 dollars in wealth for each dollar of invested equity is unquestionably impressive. Now you have a business having equity valued at \$1,462,500, meaning you have made \$1,212,500 in EMVA over your initial \$250,000 equity investment, and have achieved millionaire status with a single, high-performing restaurant.

The Case Study V-Formula
EMVA Creation

$$(2 \times 20\% - 75\% \times 9\% - 4\%) \div 25\% = 117\%$$

Equity Valuation Multiple = 117% ÷ 20%, or 5.85X

EMVA Creation = Equity Valuation Multiple – 1, or 4.85X

EMVA Contribution as a Percent of Equity Valuation
= 4.85X ÷ 5.85X, or 82.9%

What started out in the last chapter as a restaurant business model has now become a universal business performance and valuation model centered on relative numeric relationships.

Solving for Other V-Formula Variables

Any formula that can be done one way can be done backwards to solve for other variables. What if, for example, you wanted to invert your V-Formula to solve for the desired amount of OPM needed to achieve a required rate of return of 60%? In such a case, you could reduce your use of OPM from 75% in the preceding formula to just 47.1%, as follows:

V-Formula in Reverse
Determining the Desired Amount of OPM

(Sales ÷ Business Investment × Operating Profit Margin
*– **Current Pre-Tax ROE Target** – Annual Maintenance CapEx ÷ Investment)*
÷
*(Cost of OPM – **Current Pre-Tax ROE Target**)*
or
$$(2 \times 20\% - 60\% - 4\%) \div (9\% - 60\%) = 47.1\%$$

V Formula Variation
Determining OPM Interest Coverage

(Sales ÷ Business Investment × Operating Profit Margin
− Annual Maintenance CapEx ÷ Business Investment)
÷
(% of OPM × Interest Payment)
or
$(2 \times 20\% - 4\%) \div (47.1\% \times 9\%) = 8.49$

V-Formula variants can be made to solve for desired business investment, operating profit margin, or OPM cost as well. One common metric businesspeople use to determine corporate risk is the ability to cover interest payments on OPM to arrive at an interest coverage ratio. Yes, there is a V-Formula variant for that, too!

As seen above, your company's current pre-tax cash flow could cover your interest and lease payments by 8.49X, which is extremely healthy. If we were to revert to the original example of your restaurant described in the prior chapter, using 75% OPM, a 2% annual maintenance capex spend, and a 1.5 sales-to-business investment ratio, you would still have a terrific interest coverage ratio of 4.1X. For reference, private company interest coverage ratios tend to hover in an area nearer to 2X.

Would it be possible for you to achieve Mort's Model and use just OPM and no equity? The answer is yes. If you took the initial restaurant business model at the beginning of this chapter and found a way to have OPM fund the full $1 million in business investment, your payment would be $90,000 and your restaurant would still throw off $190,000 annually in pre-tax cash flow, equating to an interest coverage ratio of 3.1X. The key would be getting someone to put up all the money (and at the same interest/lease rate), which is no simple task.

A fixed charge coverage ratio is a more important cousin to the ratio of interest coverage. This ratio computes the amount of times your company can meet its annual OPM payment obligations from operating cash flow. The difference between payments and interest is the amount of principal that must be paid. If you simply take the sum of your payments and divide them into the amount of OPM obtained, you will arrive at what is called a *payment constant*, which will be higher than the 9% interest/lease rate. If you were to use that payment constant in the denominator of the preceding formula, rather than the interest rate on OPM, you would arrive at a corporate fixed charge coverage ratio.

V-Formula Data Tables

I love data tables. In Excel, you can select to use one or two variables, which is my general preference. Of the six V-Formula variables, business leaders tend to focus the most attention on the first three. Sales, business investment, and operating profit margin are the biggest contributors to current equity returns. They are the Big Three variables. Of these, the first two (as we saw earlier) can be combined into a single efficiency ratio of sales to business investment. This means that you can make a two variable data table that incorporates the Big Three V-Formula variables as follows:

Current Pre-Tax ROE

Sales: Business Investment

Operating Profit Margin	1	1.25	1.5	1.75	2
15.0%	25.0%	40.0%	55.0%	70.0%	85.0%
17.5%	35.0%	52.5%	70.0%	87.5%	105.0%
20.0%	45.0%	65.0%	**85.0%**	105.0%	125.0%
22.5%	55.0%	77.5%	100.0%	122.5%	145.0%
25.0%	65.0%	90.0%	115.0%	140.0%	165.0%

The sales to business investment ratio of our restaurant starts out at 1.5:1, with an operating profit margin of 20%. The result is an 85% current pre-tax equity rate of return. Raise the ratio to 2:1 as illustrated earlier in this chapter, and you arrive at a current pre-tax equity rate of return of 125%. Raise the operating profit margin to 25%, while keeping the sales-business investment ratio at 2:1, and you now achieve a current pre-tax equity return of 165%.

Given that we have taken a restaurant business model introduced in the prior chapter, reduced it to the Six Variables formula, and then taken away the numbers, what remains is a Six Variable universal business model. So, the preceding table, given our remaining three V-Formula variables, effectively represents a universal business model truth when it comes to current ROE estimation. If you were to create but a single universal business model two-variable data table, this would be it.

Of course, behind the preceding data table is another important two-variable data table to estimate the equity value multiple of a business. Equity value multiples are the starting point for EMVA estimation, which is the measure of business wealth creation. In this case, the two variables used are simply the current pre-tax ROE and the current pre-tax ROE hurdle rate, which is the current return other investors would expect given investments having similar growth prospects and risk. In the case of the restaurant, which has a current pre-tax equity rate of return of 85% and an investor hurdle rate of 20%, the equity value multiple is 4.25X, which means the EMVA multiple is one less, or 3.25X. The blank parts of the table occur where the hurdle rates exceed the business returns, resulting in value destruction. With companies capable of growing operating profits rapidly, the Gordon Growth Model will tend to lessen investor hurdle rates to potentially low levels resulting in elevated equity value multiples. Like the earlier table, the equity value multiple data table is important, showing universal truths regarding the capabilities of businesses to create value.

Equity Value Multiple

Current Pre-Tax ROE

	5%	10%	20%	85%	100%
5%	1.00X	2.00X	4.00X	17.00X	20.00X
10%		1.00X	2.00X	8.50X	10.00X
15%			1.33X	5.67X	6.67X
20%			1.00X	**4.25X**	5.00X
25%				3.40X	4.00X

(Row labels: Current Pre-Tax Hurdle Rate)

When it comes to understanding the basics of corporate finance and value creation, I know of no better tool than the V-Formula. As I noted early on, there are potentially infinite ways to operate your business as you seek to elevate your corporate efficiency. But in a corporate business model, just Six Variables collaboratively work together to produce equity returns.

Chapter 6
Business Model Evaluation

Some businesses simply have better business models than others. If you want examples of companies having solid business models, the Forbes 400 list of richest Americans is a good place to start. The businesses behind the Forbes 400 list have historically possessed some of the finest models going. Not only do their V-Formula variables work in concert to deliver high equity rates of return, but the businesses are universally highly scalable. More than just scalable, they often have high levels of operating leverage, which means they can grow their impressive businesses with minimal amounts of added business investment. Finally, they can also use their scalability to address extremely large market opportunities, offering high levels of corporate growth potential. For many of them, the business investment was low to begin with and the equity investment even lower, which meant that it was easier for the founding team to keep much of the equity in the businesses that they created. Companies having the best business models generally have the potential to deliver high current equity rates of return, and can do a lot of whatever it is that they do with a great deal of business investment efficiency.

Of course, getting on the Forbes 400 list of richest Americans is hardly the only measurement of financial success. For that, the bar is substantially lower. There's "rich" and then there's "*insanely rich*." While successful restaurant operators, as in our case study, can become very wealthy, they cannot ordinarily expect to make it to the Forbes 400 list of the insanely rich.

A significant drawback of restaurant business models is that operations tend to have scale limitations, with little in the way of operating leverage. However, the returns can still be attractive, and there is the potential to create material amounts of shareholder wealth. As a result, there are plenty of restaurant professionals within the top 1% of American earnings and wealth.

STORE Capital

I have been fortunate to take public and help guide three New York Stock Exchange listed real estate investment trusts, most recently STORE Capital, where I was the founding chief executive officer for a decade following our 2011 inception. Real estate investment trusts (REITs) are simply companies that invest in real estate or real estate mortgages and pay no corporate income tax. Instead, the income we produce is taxable at our shareholder level, which is more efficient than most public companies who both pay corporate taxes and then have the dividends they pay subject to further individual taxation. The price we pay for this efficiency is that we need to follow several rules, the biggest of which is that we are required to pay out 90% of our taxable income in the form of shareholder dividends. At the end of 2019, we owned close to $10 billion in real estate, which was leased on a long-term basis to profit center tenants nationwide. During 2019, our corporate ratio of sales to business investment approximated .08, or 8% (this was our lease yield from our tenants). Our OPM amounted to about 40% of business investment, our maintenance capex was minimal, and our interest rate on the cost of borrowings (our sole source of OPM) was around 4.3%. While none of these variables stand out as that exciting, net lease companies have some of the highest operating profit margins around. Our 2019 operating profit margin was about

93%. String that all together in the V-Formula and our current rate of return on equity at cost is about 10% as follows:

STORE Capital's 2019 V-Formula

(Sales ÷ Business Investment × Operating Profit Margin − % of OPM × Interest Rate − Annual Maintenance CapEx ÷ Business Investment) = Current Pre-Tax ROE

÷

% of Equity

Or

$(8\% \times 93\% - 40\% \times 4.3\% - 0) \div 60\% = \sim 10\%$

Our total rate of return was slightly better than 10% because our contractual annual tenant rent increases came in at close to 2% annually. If I use the Gordon Growth formula and add the 2% contractual growth to the initial 8% yield, the total ROE rises to over 13%.

There are three other adjustments that can be made.

First, companies like STORE can expect to have losses arising from tenant nonperformance, which will be a drag to returns.

Second, in most years STORE was typically able to raise ROE growth by selling some of our real estate to investors happy with lower yields, and then reinvesting the money at higher current rates of return.

Third, good net-lease companies historically trade for values in excess of their underlying real estate value. I tend to view this as akin to good bank stocks, which tend to trade at values in excess of their equity at cost (this is often called "book equity"). Because STORE tended to trade at a premium to its cost, the company had the ability make an added return for its existing shareholders who participated in the spread arising from new share issuance and borrowings that had a current lower cost to STORE than the yields on the assets purchased with the money. This type of growth is referred to as "external growth," because it is enabled by newly issued equity.

For STORE and other REITs to materially grow, they need to issue new equity, since the REIT dividend requirements limit their ability to retain, reinvest, and compound corporate cash flows. During my tenure at STORE, the net expected investor return from all our activity typically amounted to around 12.5% or better annually. Assuming investors would be happy with an annual return of 9% (this approximated the 20-year annual rate of return for the FTSE NAREIT All Equity REITs Index through 2020), our EMVA from the new investments would amount to about 39% on the equity we annually deployed (12.5% ÷ 9% − 1). That equity is comprised of newly issued shares, the free cash we retained, and the recycled equity from property sales. With EMVA creation potential of nearly 40% on newly deployed equity, STORE's business model has historically been potent, while having a solid margin for error to cushion from EMVA loss.

The table that follows illustrates STORE's EMVA performance between the company's 2014 initial public offering and the end of 2019. Over that five-year period, EMVA averaged better than 40% of STORE's equity at cost. When analyzing annual EMVA growth relative to annual equity growth at cost, the median EMVA contribution was just over 30%. For the first four years, STORE's stock price relative to its reported adjusted funds from operations remained relatively stable and in the middle of our peer group, meaning that the EMVA contribution was driven by a strong business model. In 2019, STORE benefited from an elevated share valuation which served to increase EMVA. For investors, an important question to ask is to what degree is EMVA creation owed to a compelling business model, versus business valuation multiples reflecting optimistic future business model aspirations.

Looking at compound annual EMVA growth is less useful for a relatively young company like STORE. For more seasoned companies, leadership will tend to look to stability in this metric. Over time, both these important metrics should tend to be reflective equity return performance delivered by a company's potent business model fundamentals.

STORE Capital EMVA Creation Performance

($000's)

Year	Equity at Cost	2019 Weighting	Equity Market Capitalization	EMVA Created	EMVA % of Equity at Cost	Compound EMVA Growth
2011	$ 256,968	9				
2012	$ 673,252	8				
2013	$ 794,523	7				
2014	$ 1,697,879	6	$ 2,489,743	$ 791,864	46.6%	23.0%
2015	$ 2,290,096	5	$ 3,267,923	$ 977,827	42.7%	18.4%
2016	$ 2,851,293	4	$ 3,937,340	$ 1,086,047	38.1%	14.4%
2017	$ 3,700,316	3	$ 5,045,689	$ 1,345,373	36.4%	12.3%
2018	$ 4,602,013	2	$ 6,258,544	$ 1,656,531	36.0%	11.0%
2019	$ 5,402,340	1	$ 8,931,005	$ 3,528,665	65.3%	16.8%

The formula for determining compound EMVA growth is shown below and requires that you compute the weighted age of the company's equity, which will tend to be less than its chronological age. In the case of the STORE table above, you simply multiply the company's equity at cost in each year by its weighting, which is the amount of years that equity has been imbedded in overall company equity at cost. Then, for 2019, you sum up the resulting nine products and divide that amount by the sum of the nine year-end company equity balances at cost to arrive at a weighted average equity age. In the case of STORE, rapid company growth and equity issuance caused the average equity age at the end of 2019 to be just 3.23 years old, or far younger than the company's actual nine-year age.

Compound EMVA Growth Formula

$$(\text{Equity Market Value} \div \text{Equity at Cost})^{(1+N)} - 1$$

Where N = Weighted average age of equity at cost

Or

$$\text{STORE Capital 2019}: (\$8,931,005 \div \$5,402,340)^{(1+3.23)} - 1 = 16.8\%$$

There were a few REIT founders in the 2021 Forbes 400 list of wealthiest Americans, but none whose fortunes were centered in that activity. STORE had an incredibly solid business model capable of creating copious EMVA, but it was simply not good enough to propel any of our founders to the illustrious *Forbes* list. The returns are too low (well below that of our restaurant case study), the company has little operating leverage (the delivered cash flow growth per share is aided by constantly raising new equity, diluting shareholders to make new investments), there is scant scalability (how do you improve on a 93% operating profit margin?), there are constraints on the ability to use a high portion of OPM (our OPM mix was limited by credit rating constraints to approximately 40%).

(Contrast STORE with Microsoft, which went public in 1986 with revenues below $200 million. By the end of 2019, revenues had grown to over $125 billion, and the company had not issued a single added share to the public to get there.)

Finally, STORE's business investment requirement was simply too high. The real estate the company owns and leases to its tenants is expensive. This meant that to start STORE, we needed to raise a lot of money from institutional investors. Having had to trade away so much of our company to the founding institutional investors who made our business possible resulted in the founders having a very low share of personal ownership. At the end of 2019, I owned well less than 1% of our stock.

Fortunately, STORE addresses a very large market, which enabled us to materially grow the company to become a large enterprise. So, while STORE's business model had wealth creation limitations for its founders, our solid business model, coupled with the size of the company, allowed our leadership to be well within the top 1% of all Americans in terms of income and wealth. We are financial success stories.

The FAANGs

By now, you are probably forming an idea of the characteristics of a solid business model. And it should be crystal clear to you that EMVA, which lies at the root of meaningful wealth creation, can be created from many different business models. Here is my take on what makes the best business models:

Capital stack. The best business models generate the highest current rates of equity return with the least use of OPM. If you are looking at a group of companies, create V-Formulas for all of them and then set OPM to zero and equity to 100%. Using OPM adds risk to the equity investors of a business because OPM has a payment priority over equity investors. Setting OPM to zero forms the most conservative capital stack, which now is 100% equity. Setting OPM to zero also allows you to compare raw business models without the benefit of OPM in their capital stacks.

Equity efficiency. The best business models have the highest ratio of operating profitability to business investment, which means that they are the most efficient users of equity. The more equity efficient a company, the less its founders will lose to others when seeking added equity to fund growth. Members of the Forbes 400 tend to own high percentages of the companies that lie at the root of their wealth.

Growth with a proven business model. The best business models tend to have the highest growth potential. For a value investor like me, growth represents risk, so it helps to have growth with a business model that is already proven to be potent. Growing *into* a potent business model is a strategy that many businesses follow, but which is subject to elevated risk. From the dot-com boom and bust of the late 1990s to technology companies 20 years later, any number of public companies, having no income, have issued vast quantities of stock. Buyer beware! There is indeed risk associated with making investments in companies having limited earnings and unknown business models.

In 2013, Jim Cramer, host of the nationally televised CNBC show *Mad Money,* coined the acronym FAANG to refer to five high-growth companies that had been collectively responsible for a disproportionate share of stock market returns. By the end of 2019, those companies—Facebook, Apple, Amazon, Netflix, and Google—had collective market valuations totaling $3.9 trillion, or better than 11% of the value of all publicly listed US equities.[1] To place this amount into context, were FAANG a country, it would have been the world's tenth largest economy, situated just behind Canada.[2]

Two years after Cramer coined the FAANG acronym, Google changed its corporate name to Alphabet, which happened in concert with its transition into a technology conglomerate. The name change did not matter. The FAANG moniker stuck, and the stocks performed. In fact, over the 10-year period between 2009 and 2018, when looking at the broad market of all US publicly listed companies, the FAANGs, which delivered a better than 30% yearly return over the decade, accounted for just over 6% of total investor rates of return across the thousands of publicly traded companies.[3]

While impressive, this is actually not unusual. Over a longer 25-year period ending in 2018, just 10% of companies delivered approximately 60% of total investor returns.[4] This fact illustrates why most investors cannot beat the market and tend to be better off investing in broad index funds; they inevitably miss out on most or all the 10%. This fact also illustrates how impressive are the track records of investors like Warren Buffett, who have shown that they can beat the market over a long period of time.

Here is what the 2019 V-Formula looks like when applied to the FAANG stocks:

	Facebook	Apple	Amazon	Netflix	Google
Sales/Business Investment	0.57	0.93	1.35	0.77	0.57
Operating Profit Margin	50.9%	32.9%	17.1%	16.9%	70.8%
% OPM	8.5%	46.5%	40.6%	69.9%	15.4%
OPM Interest Rate	6.0%	1.0%	6.2%	4.6%	5.4%
CapEx/Business Investment	9.8%	4.3%	6.2%	0.7%	7.0%
2019 Pre-Tax ROE	20.8%	48.5%	24.0%	30.2%	38.2%
After-Tax ROE (Using Reported Tax Rate)	15.5%	40.8%	19.9%	27.3%	36.0%

When you are wading through the public financial information of very large companies, the exercise will be imperfect, but will not be that far off. You may be thinking, for instance, that these companies can generally borrow at cheaper interest rates than I've shown, and you would be right. However, they also lease real estate, in some cases a lot. I ignore non-cash assets and liabilities, such as "the right to use," and concoct my own estimate. Here, I divided the annual lease expenses by my estimate of a lease rate (I used 6%) in order to approximate the value of the employed real estate that they lease but could have potentially owned. The rate I selected is based on long-run reported net lease transaction averages. For capex, I averaged the companies' annual capex over the past three years, which was derived from their respective statement of cash flows. The amount I used is probably excessive, since much of the capex they report enables them to grow and is not simply maintenance capex. In determining cash operating profit margins, I backed out the non-cash stock-based compensation. But if you look at the statements of shareholder equity, you can figure out that the equity dilution from employee stock awards tends to range from roughly .5% to 1.5% annually, which you can simply strike from the current pre-tax equity rates of return.

Finally, the reported income tax rates of the five companies varied from a low of 6% for Google to a high of about 25% for Facebook. These are excluded from the V-Formula and would lower the current equity returns of these tax-paying companies illustrated in the above table.

The impressiveness of the FAANG group is partly evident in the sheer amount of cash on their balance sheets. Elevated cash balances are a two-edged sword; they give investors comfort but depress returns because they inflate the business investment V-Formula variable. At the end of 2019, Netflix was sitting on just over $5 billion, which was the lowest cash balance of the five. Apple reported over $200 billion in cash, Google over $100 billion, and Facebook and Amazon over $50 billion each. If you were thinking about how many days of sales their cash represents, the answer would be:

Days Sales in Cash

12-31-2019

Apple – 288	Netflix – 91
Facebook – 283	Amazon – 71
	Google – 270

If I were to make all the FAANGs have Amazon's 71 days of sales in cash, the revised V-Formula would suggest the following current pre-tax equity returns.

Adjusted for 71 Days Sales in Cash	Facebook	Apple	Amazon	Netflix	Google
Sales/Business Investment	0.86	2.11	1.35	0.80	0.82
Operating Profit Margin	50.9%	32.9%	17.1%	16.9%	70.8%
% OPM	12.8%	105.0%	40.7%	72.9%	22.3%
OPM Interest Rate	6.0%	1.0%	6.2%	4.6%	5.4%
CapEx/Business Investment	14.6%	9.7%	6.3%	0.7%	10.1%
2019 Pre-Tax ROE	32.7%	∞	24.0%	35.0%	60.2%

With the reduced business investment arising from lower cash balances, the FAANGs (excepting Amazon) all post better ratios of sales to business investment.

Also helpful in the elevated current ROE computations is keeping the use of OPM constant. We're doing this exercise for illustrative purposes, and such an elevation in the use of OPM may not be realistic because corporate access to borrowings and the corporate cost of borrowings may be facilitated by having large cash balances. In fact, the reduction in Apple's cash balances is so material it causes OPM to actually exceed total business investment, allowing the company to realize Mort's Model! The one drag from reducing cash balances is in the form of capex, which stays constant and is therefore higher as a percentage of the reduced business investment.

Each of these companies is impressive, producing high levels of current equity rates of return, together with the historic growth and return compounding typically delivered by scalable business models. Large amounts of cash on the balance sheets of Apple, Google, and Facebook served to materially elevate their business investments and depress returns. The cash also poses an investor risk to the extent that it is deployed into future business expansions having inferior returns to those delivered by these companies from their historic operations.

Now, how do these five companies look if we set their OPM variable to zero?

Adjusted OPM Set to Zero	Facebook	Apple	Amazon	Netflix	Google
Sales/Business Investment	0.57	0.93	1.35	0.77	0.57
Operating Profit Margin	50.9%	32.9%	17.1%	16.9%	70.8%
% OPM	0.0%	0.0%	0.0%	0.0%	0.0%
OPM Interest Rate	6.0%	1.0%	6.2%	4.6%	5.4%
CapEx/Business Investment	9.8%	4.3%	6.2%	0.7%	7.0%
2019 Pre-Tax ROE	19.5%	26.4%	16.8%	12.3%	33.2%

Eliminating OPM lowers current equity rates of return. As the user of the most OPM, Netflix's returns fall by almost two-thirds, from 30.2% to 12.3%. Apple and Amazon are next, falling by approximately 45% and 30%, respectively. Google and Facebook employ comparatively little in the way of OPM, and their returns are not largely impacted. Interestingly, Facebook, Apple, and Google made so little use of OPM and maintained so much cash that eliminating borrowings would not lessen their current corporate size. The same could not be said of Amazon or Netflix, which would have to lessen their business investments by approximately 15% and 50%, respectively.

Based on this analysis and the prior adjusted cash balance analysis, Apple and Google have financial business models that stand out in a collectively impressive group.

The above exercises are interesting. There are just Six Variables, but you can see how diverse corporate business models can be. The FAANGs may be grouped together, but their business models vary.

You may be wondering how the FAANG V-Formula analysis might apply to your personal decision to invest in these companies. Well, the model is a start, but has two drawbacks as an investment tool.

The first of these is that the model is completely quantitative. Any investment decision must also be qualitative.

Second, and importantly, the V-Formula illustrates the corporate returns on each company's equity investment *at cost*. While the founders of these five companies were able to buy in at cost, that opportunity is lost to you. At the end of 2019, each of the FAANGs traded at substantial premiums to their cost to create, which meant that the current equity rates of return for new shareholders would have been substantially less.

I estimate that the cost of Apple's equity at the end of its 2019 fiscal year was $149 billion. Embedded in that large number is a small one: the original investment cobbled together by co-founders Steve Jobs and Steve Wozniak and the subsequent venture capital investment in their company that followed after they invented the Apple II computer in 1976, which made them millionaires. In

December 1980, Apple was taken public on the fledgling NASDAQ market, selling under 10% of its corporate shares for over $100 million in the largest IPO since Ford Motor Company in 1956. Between then and the end of 2019, Apple did not issue additional shares, but split its shares four times. (A split is when a company gives its shareholders added shares of stock while lowering the price of each share to maintain the immediate collective share value.) As a result, had you purchased 10 shares of Apple stock in 1980 at a price of $22 per share, you would own approximately 560 shares at the end of 2019 valued at almost $165,000, for an 18.5% compound rate of return, excluding dividends.

As good as you would have done owning Apple shares since 1980, the founders and early private investors did far better, retaining over 90% of the shares at a far lower investment price per share in the company that they helped start. At the end of 2019, the company's equity was valued at an amount almost 10 times greater than its cost, catapulting Apple to be the first technology company ever to

Steve Jobs, Apple Co-Founder, in front of the garage of his childhood home in Los Altos, CA where Apple was conceived. The house is now designated as a historic site.
Credit: Diane Cook and Len Jenshel / Getty Images

have an equity valuation greater than $1 trillion. About $900 billion of that equity valuation represented EMVA.

From a V-Formula perspective as illustrated earlier, Apple at the end of 2019 was impressive. However, the company's current pre-tax equity rate of return would have been unavailable to you, since to buy shares in each company you would have to pay a multiple of approximately 10 times the original equity cost.

In paying such a high premium over the cost to create a company, can the V-Formula still help you understand if the investment is attractive? The answer is yes.

Chapter 7
Pulling the Corporate Efficiency Levers

The Six Variables that drive corporate shareholder returns can be grouped into three types of corporate financial efficiency. At a high level, these efficiencies represent the financial levers at the hands of management that will impact future corporate equity returns and shareholder value creation. The three types of corporate financial efficiency are:

1. Operating efficiency (O)
2. Asset efficiency (A)
3. Capital efficiency (C)

Although all three efficiencies are equally important, most businesspeople I know tend to focus on corporate efficiencies in pretty much this order. The V-Formula numerator contains the Six Variables that can pretty much be divided evenly into the three corporate efficiencies.

The formula denominator, being just the percentage of the business funded by equity, is not an added variable; it is just the inverse of the percentage of the business funded by OPM.

Here is the V-Formula numerator, with each variable labeled with the type of corporate efficiency it represents:

Operating Efficiency O			**Asset Efficiency A**	**Capital Efficiency C**	
O	A	O	C	C	A&O	A

Sales ÷ Business Investment × Operating Profit Margin − % of OPM × Cost of OPM − Maintenance CapEx ÷ Business Investment

Operating Efficiency (O)

Sales

Corporate operating efficiency begins with sales. A banking adage that I learned at the beginning of my career is this: "No one ever went out of business because they had too many sales." Sales are the life blood of a business, the first key to corporate operating efficiency, and are effectively simplified in the V-Formula. That's because sales, like all Six Variables, can be expanded upon. An expanded formula for sales might look like this:

Sales

(Number of Customers

×

Average Price of Products You Sell

×

Average Number of Products Bought by Each Customer)

The V-Formula is a universal simplification that can be easily expanded. Given the above example, we could eliminate the sales variable altogether, replacing the single variable with the three components that comprise sales above. As we will see in this chapter, each of the Six Variables can be likewise expanded, which would result in a far longer, more complex formula. That said, the math would still be basic middle school math, which is a good thing from the vantage point of most entrepreneurs, since most of us never set out to be math wizards.

Behind the three variables comprising sales is one more: The number of different products you sell. In theory, the bigger your product line, the more customers you might be able to get and the greater the number of products an average customer might buy. You may also be able to charge a higher price for the convenience of having so many products.

Of course, in some cases, reality can be different. For instance, if you are a restaurant operator, more products will require a larger menu. Larger menus increase operating complexity, inventory needs, and likely raise the level of food waste.

In 1988, Wendy's, the nation's third largest fast-food hamburger chain, rolled out its Superbar, which was an expanded salad bar that included salad, fruit, Mexican fare, and even pasta. The idea was to raise customer counts through an expanded product offering. Franchisees were expected to shell out dollars to install the Superbars, which took up space that reduced dining area seating capacity. The effort at product offering expansion turned out to be an operational and gastronomic train wreck. Operators struggled with the elevated labor needs to manage the Superbar. Food costs, which are centered in portion management, were harder to control. So was food waste, which increased due to the need to constantly refresh food bar offerings. In this process, the chain saw its well-earned reputation for quality suffer. Ultimately, this impacted overall same-store sales, operating profitability, and the company's share price. In 1998, after a decade of struggle, the company pulled the Superbars and successfully turned to menu simplification.

The inspiration behind restaurant menu expansion is typically to limit the "veto vote." Basically, the theory is that broad menu offerings will reduce the possibility that one member of a group—the family on vacation, for example—will express dislike for the menu and compel the group to look elsewhere, thereby losing several sales. But the lesson from Wendy's product expansion efforts is that sometimes it's better *not* to spend precious money and resources chasing every conceivable sale. Many restaurant chains have successfully implemented product strategies that entail limited offerings. McDonald's and Domino's began that way, and Chick-fil-A and In-N-Out Burger, with four members of the elite 2021 Forbes 400 list of wealthiest Americans among them, are two current examples of restaurant chains that successfully adhere to strategies grounded in limited menu offerings.

Operating Profit Margin

The second corporate efficiency variable is operating profit margin. Part of operating profit margin is simply impacted by the first component of the sales variable, which is product price. Assuming all else equal, if product prices are raised, then the corporate profit margin will go up. In reality, most companies in our competitive economy find they have limited pricing power. But you can see corporate efforts to earn pricing power everywhere. Branding is a clear example. When Daymond John created FUBU, he created a brand that people wanted to own, believing it to be more valuable. The sleek, appealing designs offered by Apple have long made its products aspirational, enabling comparatively higher pricing and elevated profit margins. Likewise, retailers often have private label merchandise affixed with their logos to elevate pricing power through branding and the appearance of scarcity (you can't find the exact same merchandise anywhere else). Unquestionably, aspirational luxury goods makers have invested a great deal in elevating brand awareness that confers pricing power.

Most business efforts to elevate profit margins involve cost control. If you are selling a retail or manufactured product, you might first look at managing your *cost of goods sold*. For many companies, this is their single largest cost. Walmart, the world's single largest retail chain, with annual revenues exceeding $500 billion annually as of January 2020, operates on notoriously thin margins. Between their fiscal years ending January 31, 2017, and January 31, 2020, gross profit margins (this is simply equal to [sales – cost of goods sold] ÷ sales) approximated 25%. No doubt, a great deal of effort is expended by the company to reduce its cost of goods sold and thereby elevate its gross profit margins. The sum of Walmart's operating and general and administrative costs amounted to about 21% of sales, or less than a third of their cost of goods sold. Doubtless, the company had initiatives in place to manage these costs also. That would be natural because their net income margin (reported net income divided into sales) averaged below 2% between 2017 and 2020. This kind of statistic makes Walmart a poster child for high volume, low margin companies. With profit margins this low, if you think you are getting a good deal at Walmart, you generally are.

As we discussed earlier in Chapter 4, operating profit margin is simply EBITDAR as a percentage of sales. However, in keeping with the thought that V-Formula variables are each expandable to elevate detail, a high-level formula for operating profit margin for Walmart might look like this:

Operating Profit Margin

1 − (((Cost of Goods Sold

+

Operating, General Administrative Expenses)

÷

Sales)

Consistent with our financial approach, within the definition of EBITDAR (earnings before interest, taxes, depreciation, and rents), non-cash accounting conventions like depreciation and executive stock compensation are excluded from the formula. Also, lease costs for assets that might otherwise have been purchased are frequently included in operating expenses. I remove these costs as I try to make a more accurate assessment of the percentage of a company funded by OPM.

However, it should be clear by now that you can make this operating profit formula as long as you wish. You can break out specific goods costs or specific operating and general and administrative expenses. You might choose to do this to note the large costs that bear the most attention. By making single variable formulas for sales or operating profit margin into multiple variables, the simplified universal business model that is the V-Formula becomes far more tailored.

Asset Efficiency (A)

Business Investment

Asset (or business investment) efficiency is simply the notion of working to make your business investment as low as possible. All else equal, the less money tied up in business investment, the better. If you are operating the restaurant in our case study, you might attempt to see if you can construct the restaurant for less. I have helped finance thousands of restaurant properties and have occasionally seen companies desiring to build expensive monuments to gastronomy when smaller, more efficient facilities will do. Overbuilding requires little talent. Rather, the talent lies in crafting prudent construction budgets that deliver well-built facilities looking like you spent more than they cost. Or you might see if you can rent another property cheaply enough to represent an effective price discount over the cost of new construction. In such a case, you might even see if your landlord would pay for most or all the necessary conversion costs.

While the business investment of restaurant companies tends to be dominated by real estate, furniture, fixtures, and equipment costs, other business models entail significant investments in working capital assets, which include accounts receivable, inventory, and prepaid and deferred costs. This is especially so for manufacturing companies like FUBU or Apple, which tend to have every type of working capital asset imaginable. Retailers like Walmart will likewise have lots of dollars invested in inventory, but tend to have little in the way of accounts receivable; their customers pay by cash or credit card, which means that retailers tend to experience minimal delay between the time they sell their merchandise and the time they are paid for it.

What follows is a basic formula for the business investment V-Formula variable. As with the sales and operating profit margin variables, you can expand this variable to include the "hard asset" variables as well as a myriad of "working capital" variables that collectively comprise business investment. In this way, a universal business variable (business investment) can be custom-tailored to your business.

Business Investment

Hard Asset Variables

(Land, Building, Furniture, Fixtures and Equipment You Buy &
Land Building, Furniture, Fixtures and Equipment You Could Buy, but Rent

& Working Capital Variables

+ (Accounts Receivable, Inventory, Cash Balances, Prepaid & Deferred Costs)
− (Accounts Payable, Accrued Expenses, Deferred Income, Deposits & Other 0 − Cost Liabilities))

In our global economy, supply chain management has become a specialization and is at the heart of business efforts to limit their amount of working capital by speeding up the cash flow cycle. (You may recall Daymond John's initial onerous 240-day revenue cycle.) Inventory can be maintained at low levels through restocking strategies that entail inventory that is delivered "just in time." Terms of customer accounts receivable can be shortened. Requirements for the prepayment of inventory or services can be limited. Vendor accounts payable terms can be lengthened. Customer deposits can be requested on orders. Indeed, there are a lot of working capital levers that can be addressed. Not surprisingly, given the increased level of attention to working capital demands, your efforts to reduce working capital will conflict with similar incentives on the parts of your suppliers and the businesses you sell to.

Supply chain management and a global economy have contributed to advances in business model efficiency. Perhaps the biggest of these is for companies to elect "asset-light" operating models. Think of Apple, where merchandise labels note that devices are "designed by Apple in California," but made globally through a sophisticated supplier network. As a result, Apple has fewer requirements for real estate, furniture, fixtures, and equipment, which lowers their business investment needs and trades off high levels of associated fixed operating costs for variable production costs. Likewise, clothing manufacturers such as FUBU have the potential to limit their expenditures to the design elements of their business, outsourcing production and distribution. Through such efforts, the aim is to achieve a business model requiring less cash to create, resulting in less OPM and less YOM while delivering a high level of scalability and the potential for elevated equity returns and wealth creation.

Operating leverage is the ability to materially grow sales without similar added investments in hard assets. Operating leverage tends to be a common characteristic of companies capable of high levels of EMVA creation. Still, even with such companies, working capital business investment requirements will tend to rise commensurately with sales. For working capital intensive businesses, the downside of sales growth is a loss of cash that might otherwise have been used for other investments or contemplated investor cash distributions. How much can sales grow before you need additional equity infusion to support working capital? The answer is approximately the same sales growth as your current rate of after-tax current equity returns, which is also what is called your "sustainable growth rate." Here, it's worth noting that added working capital business investment can be driven by either real or inflationary sales growth, which serves as a reminder of the destructive impacts of inflation.

Early on in my banking career, I recall looking at a successful Latin American retailer based in a country having a very high rate of inflation at the time. The resultant working capital growth left the company in a cash trap requiring continued inflation-driven business investment producing no real added value. For working capital intensive companies, added business investment will accompany sales growth, whether it is real of inflationary.

Notably absent from the computation of business investment are research and development (R&D) costs, which are central to technology-centric companies. Without question, R&D activities are absolutely an investment in the future, but they are typically not shown as balance sheet assets. They are instead expensed, impacting operating profit margins and operating efficiency, as opposed to business investment and asset efficiency. This characterization can potentially serve to understate equity rates of return, assuming you believe your R&D costs to be investments having real long-term value that will translate into future revenues.

In a nutshell, that is what business investment is: Assets *essential to revenue creation* that are funded by OPM and equity. Therefore, in determining your V-Formula, you might consider the inclusion of R&D costs as a business investment while removing them from operating expenses. Or you can take a more conservative approach by including R&D costs as operating expenditures, which will serve to compress your operating profit margin and lessen calculated equity returns.

Choosing how to best incorporate R&D costs into your current equity return analysis mirrors accounting imperfection. On the one hand, GAAP demands that R&D costs be expensed when they are made. On the other hand, when a company having made such R&D investments is acquired by another company, it is acceptable to capitalize the proven value of trademarks and patents into business investment. In other words, the accounting profession permits capitalization, but only in the context of an acquisition after the R&D expenses have demonstrated their long-term value.

Maintenance CapEx

Within the V-Formula, there is one other variable that impacts both asset and operating efficiency. That variable is the amount paid annually for maintenance capex. Regular maintenance capex is simply the amount you spend on hard assets annually to maintain the existing business you have. If you elect to include R&D costs in your definition of business investment, you would then include any replacement R&D costs in your annual maintenance capex costs to maintain product relevancy. Typically, businesses will expend far more on R&D or hard asset investments than just annual capital maintenance capex, but much of this will be in the form of expansion-related investments, which is an added form of business investment. We will discuss funding added business investment in a later chapter.

When it comes to the notion of maintenance capex, I tend to include two other forms of annual expenditure. The first of these is what I call *periodic remodeling costs*, which are mostly evident in consumer-facing businesses. Every five years or so, retailers, hotel operators, fitness clubs and many more businesses will undergo a reimaging or remodeling to maintain an up-to-date look and feel of the business. Without such periodic extensive remodeling, consumer-facing businesses generally risk the loss of customers to competing businesses boasting a better appearance. Hence, if you are in such a business, you should factor into your annual maintenance capex variable the average annual cost of a more material periodic reinvestment requirement.

In addition to the cost of periodic extensive remodels, I might also include the costs associated with *poor decisions*. Throughout most of my career, I have worked extensively with multilocation consumer-facing businesses. One lesson I have learned from this is the amount of sales generated by each location seldom correlates to the cost to construct that location. As a result of this unpredictability, there tends to be a location failure rate that will exact a cost on the business model. Nearly every well-known multilocation, consumer-facing company has experienced location closures. Sometimes such closures arise from facility relocation, in which case the losses from old location dispositions are probably best included as an addition to the cost of business investment for the replacement location. Even the best retailers suffer periodic store relocations and closures. During 2016, Walmart closed nearly 300 locations. Some years before that, the company's growth strategy entailed the development of larger Walmart Supercenters, together with the closure and divestiture of older, smaller store prototypes.

> # Maintenance CapEx
>
> (Annual Maintenance CapEx
>
> +
>
> Average Annual Periodic Remodeling Cost
>
> +
>
> Average Annual Losses Arising from Closures or Relocations)

Of course, business investment failures are not simply associated with multilocation consumer facing retail and service companies. Technology companies will likewise occasionally light R&D money on fire. And companies seeking to expand through M&A activity invariably will make some poor investments.

Maintenance capex is not generally the most material variable within the V-Formula. However, it can highlight business investment tradeoffs. At a basic level, those tradeoffs could be between the hard asset portion of business investment and the cost to maintain those very assets over time. Or there can be tradeoffs between corporate expansion strategies requiring new business investment and the potential wealth destruction risks of poor decisions.

Capital Efficiency (C)

OPM Variables

Cost of capital refers to the weighted cost of equity and OPM. The idea is that, by achieving the lowest cost of capital, the company will be worth more, and shareholders (company founders and early investors foremost) will be the beneficiaries. The logic sounds circular, since a higher mix of OPM will raise equity returns while potentially elevating corporate risk through higher leverage, which can raise the cost of equity. This is why Franco Modigliani and Merton Miller, while they were professors at Carnegie Mellon University in 1958, developed what is often called the "Capital Structure Irrelevance Principle," which essentially stated that varying mixes of OPM and equity would have no impact on corporate valuations. The theorem would contribute to their eventual recognition by the Royal Swedish Academy of Sciences, which in 1985 awarded Modigliani the Nobel Prize in Economics, and then in 1990 the same prize for Miller.

Key theorem assumption exclusions included taxes and transaction costs and included the assumption that individuals and corporations borrow money at the same rates. In the real world, these limitations are violated constantly. Tax considerations are frequent, individuals and companies do not borrow at the same rates, and OPM is hardly a consistent commodity for the vast number of private American businesses.

1985 Nobel Laureate Franco Modigiani and 1990 Nobel Laureate Merton Miller, creators of the "Capital Structure Irrelevance Principle"

A company's cost of capital can be lowered in many ways. Diversified loan conduits, which are basically pools of loans sold to fixed-income investors, can enable businesses to borrow at investment-grade rates, even though they might not otherwise be corporately rated BBB– or higher, which is the definition of investment-grade. This technology is akin to the ability of the average American to obtain a low-cost home mortgage because of the diversity of residential mortgage loan pools and the perceived safety of residential real estate. The availability of tools like loan conduits or whole business securitizations, whereby valuable corporate assets are pledged in the process of investment-grade debt issuance, is one reason that comparatively few companies globally bother to have investment-grade corporate credit ratings. Likewise, preferred stocks, convertible debt, and convertible preferred shares are sophisticated forms of OPM, often delivered by investors having an ability to offer competitive capital pricing enabled by diversification. Corporate real estate locations, aircraft, and other long-term assets can be efficiently leased rather than owned. The most recent company I co-founded, STORE Capital, provides such services for real estate. While leasing tends to have a higher cost than borrowing, lease solutions can lower capital costs because they enable the use of less shareholder equity. At the same time, leasing tends to free up cash flow, because it has amongst the lowest payment constants available with long-term OPM. This is because leasing companies are often not expecting you to repay the proceeds used to acquire the property and are willing to undertake residual ownership risk.

Leasing companies, especially those that lease equipment, often derive tax benefits from their property ownership, which can contribute to the efficiency of this type of OPM. Beyond this, leasing solutions can often serve to deliver more financial flexibility, which is also highly important in determining your optimal capital stack. Corporate flexibility is essential to avoid *opportunity costs,* which are essentially corporate activity limitations that have the potential to exact a price. Opportunity costs are an important business consideration and will be discussed later in greater detail.

OPM Variables

% of OPM (Interest − Costing Borrowings + Interest − Costing Lease Proceeds) ÷ Business Investment	×	Cost of OPM (Interest + Lease Payments) ÷ (Interest − Costing Borrowings + Interest − Costing Lease Proceeds)

Since the Modigliani-Miller theorem—the Capital Structure Irrelevance Principle—was conceived in 1958, capital markets have advanced greatly, and companies like STORE have emerged with the promise of effecting lower corporate costs of capital. The Capital Structure Irrelevance Principle fundamentally posited (with important assumption limitations) that there is no free lunch. However, it turns out that the theorem's limiting assumptions are not limited in the real world, meaning that there actually is free lunch to be had. It's up to business leaders to uncover such opportunities, and thereby raise equity returns and wealth creation potential.

Six-Shot Economics

The Six Variables in the V-Formula can be apportioned between a company's operating, asset, and capital efficiencies. In turn, those Six Variables can be expanded to include 30 or more variables, raising the complexity of the V-Formula as you tailor it to your enterprise. I have historically referred to the six basic financial efficiency levers as "Six-Shot Economics," being broadly the universal financial tools at the hands of business leadership that offer six shots to elevate equity returns and wealth creation.[1]

Six-Shot Economics is driven by constant innovation. Within a highly competitive global marketplace, the pace of innovation places greater demands upon business leaders and their teams to constantly modify their six efficiency levers.

Like any economic concept, the implications of Six-Shot Economics span from the micro corporate level to macro implications for economies as a whole. As business leadership takes more shots at corporate efficiencies, the impact of these collective efforts across millions of businesses is bound to contribute to improved economic growth, accompanied by elevated productivity and controlled inflation. So, more than just a financial toolkit for business leaders, Six-Shot Economics contributes meaningfully to our overall prosperity and economic health.

Chapter 8
Choosing from Your OPM Options

Capital stack assembly is a key part of the creativity involved in building a business. There can be a seemingly endless array of options to choose from. Still, as we discussed earlier in chapter 3, there is an order of operations in striving for capital efficiency that can help make sense of your options.

First things first: Begin with OPM. Here, I am referring to interest-paying OPM. If you don't have enough YOM, you can also use forms of OPM to help with equity requirements, which we will discuss later.

Then, when it comes to selecting from OPM options, there is another order of operations: Begin with the longest-term financing you can find. Longer term financings will tend to have lower payment constants, which, as a reminder, represent the relationship between the amount of OPM received and the annual payments required. Low payment constants can be more important than low interest rates. The lower the payment, the greater the free cash flow. The greater the free cash flow, the better the equity returns and the greater the odds of getting close to Mort's Model. The greater the free cash flow, the bigger your margin of safety.

With so many OPM options to select from, how do you go about choosing the right capital stack for you? This chapter will help guide you through an analytical framework that will help you decide.

Purely for illustrative purposes, I will focus on real estate financing decisions, since it is the asset most in my experiential strike zone. Companies I have helped lead have been characterized by business investments centered in real estate that we have had to fund with OPM. Equally important, our real estate investments have likewise represented a form of real estate OPM for our many tenants and borrowers.

Designing Your Own OPM

Sometimes it helps to imagine OPM attributes that you would *ideally* like to see. In my own personal business career, I have occasionally been able to put together OPM from scratch that suited our corporate objectives. Given that you don't always have to order off the menu, what would represent the ideal form of real estate finance capital for you?

When it comes to real estate OPM, my answer is that I would want to own my properties using fully financed (100% OPM), interest-only, assumable, 30-year financing, with a fixed interest rate priced competitively with the lowest interest rates available on commercial mortgage loans.

I would also like to have the option to prepay the loan at any time with little or no prepayment penalty. Personal fixed rate home mortgages can typically be prepaid or refinanced with no prepayment penalty, but such is generally not the case with commercial real estate loans.

Finally, I would like to have no loan covenants, which lenders often impose on businesses as a means of setting corporate performance guardrails, thereby steering companies to maintain a consistent credit quality profile over the long term. As a businessperson who has generally taken a conservative approach toward company construction, covenants are generally not a problem. However,

I have seen covenants restrict corporate behavior in ways that have limited the potential for greater wealth creation. In business, this is classified as an opportunity cost, which can be an unfortunate byproduct of covenants, debt prepayment costs, and other restrictions imposed by OPM providers.

If my wish list for real estate financing seems aggressive, it is. However, you might be surprised to know that we came close to providing such financing for the chain store real estate sectors our first public company addressed. Over a four-year span between 1995 and 1998, we and several other companies were able to offer fixed-rate, prepayable, assumable, 20-year, 100% financing to our customers.

Then, two things happened. First, one of the world's largest and most highly leveraged hedge funds, Long-Term Capital Management, imploded in 1998 as a result of investment bets that went wrong in wake of Asian and Russian currency devaluations. The result for us of this major market disruption was a rise in the cost of our borrowings and an inability to economically offer freely prepayable loans. (Our debt investors—our source of OPM—began to require costly prepayment restrictions, which we had to pass on to our customers.) Secondly, not long afterwards, most of the companies we competed against ceased operations as a result of poor portfolio performance. We fared better, but the product ultimately became too costly to provide. As I write, there is no such thing as 100% advance rate, prepayable, assumable, fixed-rate real estate mortgage capital for virtually any type of commercial real estate.

Leasing

Long-lived, hard assets like real estate generally have a second type of available OPM: You can *lease* them. With an inability to own and ideally finance the real estate I use in my business, what might be my ideal real estate *leasing* terms?

To begin with, I would assume the landlord would be providing all the capital for the cost of the real estate. With a 100% advance rate on the real estate I need, I would be able to conserve equity, which would offer the possibility of elevated equity returns and wealth creation.

Ideally, I would like to have a lease of five years or less, but one having lots of fixed price renewal options extending for 50 years or more. This would provide me with frequent options to close or relocate the real estate used in my business. Assuming I chose to keep using the real estate, the minimal lease escalations would be expected to lag the inflation rate, which would make the lease payments increasingly below market.

I would love to have a fixed-price purchase option at any time, which would enable me to potentially ultimately own the leased asset.

Finally, I would seek a lease that was completely assumable. That way, I could one day sell my business and benefit from having a partially portable capital stack that could simply be assumed.

It turns out that many of the items on the net lease wish list are available. However, when it comes to lease duration, to compensate for the risks undertaken in buying or constructing a building, most landlords will expect companies to execute leases having primary terms of 15 years or more. While purchase options are not commonplace, our companies have frequently granted tenant fair market value purchase options, providing they are within short-lived windows. For instance, we have offered options within defined periods during the tenth or fifteenth years of the lease. Our leases have generally been fully assumable without our consent, so long as a successor tenant fulfills certain financial criteria that we set forth in the lease. Of course, we can always grant permission even if the criteria are not met. In addition to these features, we have often included property substitution rights, whereby a tenant can swap out a property for another location subject to some simple criteria. This can give a tenant added flexibility to shutter an underperforming location. Substitution rights can also help save tenants from landlords who are unable to pay for the expansion of outperforming locations: Simply swap out the property for an equivalent location and then find another landlord or OPM to fund the expansion of the outperforming location.

Creating a Model to Evaluate OPM Options

Given various OPM options for your real estate, one can lay out a financial model to determine what is right for you. Not long after we started STORE in 2011, I created a brief V-Formula-driven financial model that compared financing real estate with leasing real estate. We placed the model on STORE's website so that companies could better evaluate their real estate capital choices. Here are the basic financial model inputs:

Model Assumptions	
Income Statement	
Sales	$1,500,000
Annual Sales Growth	2.0%
EBITDAR Margin	20.0%
Real Estate Lease	
Cap Rate (RE)	8.5%
Rent-to-Sales Ratio	8.0%
Annual Lease Escalations	1.5%
Real Estate Debt	
Real Estate Loan-to-Value	70%
Interest Rate	6.0%
Amortization (Years)	20
Working Capital Component of Business Investment	
Working Capital/Real Estate Value (%)	15.0%

Like our initial V-Formula model, the model is simplistic. I ignored the capital need for equipment or other business investment needs at this juncture. The idea here was to isolate the real estate finance decision, which entailed two choices. I could rent the property by paying 8.5% of the landlord's real estate cost in the first year (this is called a "cap rate" in real estate terms), with such rent rising 1.5% annually thereafter. My rent as a percentage of the location's $1.5 million in sales is 8%, meaning that the real estate cost is $1,411,765 (that is to say, $1,500,000 × 8% ÷ 8.5%).

Alternatively, I can own the real estate by obtaining a loan for 70% of the property cost from a bank subject to a 6% interest rate and equal monthly payments that amortize the loan over 20 years.

Given these options, what would be my better choice? Which option creates more EMVA?

When faced with financial options, a common approach in business is to compare the annual cash flow differentials and then compute a single present value of the differentials by discounting the hypothetical future cash flows to the present using an assumed interest rate that approximates your expected equity rate of return requirement. I prefer to take a different approach and look at the decision dynamics at varying points of time.

Year 1

Pre-Tax Equity Yields	RE Lease	RE Own
Current Pre-Tax Yield on Equity[1]	85.00%	37.89%
Pre-Tax Cash Flow Equity Yield[2]	85.00%	33.85%
Sales: Investment Ratio	0.924	0.924
Investment % Funded with Equity	13.04%	39.13%

[1] EBITDA + Amount of Cash Equity Invested (which rises through debt repayment)
[2] (EBITDA – Loan Principal Payments) + Amount of Cash Equity Invested

The above table illustrates what is likely to happen in the first year. Should I elect to rent the property, my equity investment is limited to funding the small working capital component of business investment, in this case about 13%. However, should I elect to own the real estate, the 30% real estate equity requirement will elevate my overall equity contribution to almost 40% of the business investment. The result is that the current pre-tax equity returns are materially higher if I should elect to rent the real estate and use the landlord's equity rather than my own (85% vs. 37.89%). True, the cost of the lease appears far higher (8.5% vs. 6%), but the lower interest rate is no match for the elevated equity commitment I must make. Note that my cash flow equity yield from ownership is even less, due to the requirement to repay the note. In this case, a 6% interest rate, repaid over 20 years, entails a payment constant of 8.6%.

Of course, the story does not end here. Given the lease increases of 1.5% every year (versus the fixed payments on the loan amount), owning the real estate might be expected to look a bit better over time. Here is the same model output shown for the end of the fifth year:

Year 5

Pre-Tax Equity Yields	RE Lease	RE Own
Current Pre-Tax Yield on Equity[1]	93.20%	34.98%
Pre-Tax Cash Flow Equity Yield[2]	93.20%	30.56%

[1] EBITDA ÷ Amount of Cash Equity Invested (which rises through debt repayment)
[2] (EBITDA − Loan Principal Payments) ÷ Amount of Cash Equity Invested

As the years progress, it may be surprising to see that leasing looks increasingly better. Sales rise 2% annually, more than offsetting the impact of the modest 1.5% annual rent increases. For you to break even on the annual rent increase, you would have to raise your prices just .12%, which you get by multiplying the 1.5% annual rent increase by the initial 8% rent to sales relationship. Meanwhile, because of mortgage loan repayments associated with the ownership option, the equity mix associated with real estate ownership rises year after year, further depressing the comparative equity rate of return and cash flow equity yield.

There is one last important key quantitative point that bears mentioning: the amount of equity preserved, given a decision to lease. The election to own a location entails an equity investment approximating *three times* the amount that would otherwise be required to lease a location. Or, to put it another way, by choosing to own, you are foregoing the opportunity to open *two more locations*. Over a five-year period, the amount of incremental pre-tax cash

flow lost would come close to $2 million. Add in another approxi-
mate $1.5 million from the lost EMVA from the larger business (this
assumes a 20% current annual equity pre-tax rate of return hurdle
rate) and the amount lost as a result of the election to own, rather
than lease, real estate amounts to closer to $3.5 million over a five-
year period.

Capital stack elections have EMVA creation consequences!

The decision to lease seems certain to win, but there are more
considerations. For one thing, the large equity requirement associated with real estate ownership does result in higher levels of
corporate pre-tax cash flow. True, the OPM payment constant is
about the same, but the comparative equity mix from ownership is
approximately 39%, versus just 13% with the election to lease. As a
result, the margin of safety associated with the elevated cash flows
from ownership is higher. How much? The elevated equity associated with ownership enables the company to have a fixed charge
coverage ratio, which is the number of times cash flow can service
OPM obligations, of approximately 3.5X, versus 2.5X for the leasing option. The latter number is respectable, but the difference can
cause one to examine if the elevated risk associated with the higher
OPM usage will also cause potential equity investors to demand
higher rates of return.

There are three remaining quantitative issues associated with a
decision to own, rather than lease, real estate:

1. **Loss of real estate appreciation.** This is the level of real estate
   appreciation that might be forgone with an election to lease real
   estate. In electing to rent a property, rather than own it, you are
   trading a fee simple interest in real estate for a leasehold interest. Given that real estate leases in recent history generally have
   annual lease escalations capped at 2% and less, that is really all
   landlords can anticipate when it comes to long-term appreciation. This means that real estate value inflation above the lease
   escalation rate will continue to benefit the tenant.
2. **Depreciation tax shield value.** This pertains to the potential
   for real estate ownership to provide a lower marginal tax rate arising from real estate depreciation. The matter of the comparative

value of the depreciation tax shield is fairly straightforward. The benefits of real estate depreciation are not that material, since the building and improvements are generally ratably expensed over a 39-year period. Plus, given the higher use of OPM with a decision to lease, the amount of taxable income would generally be the same.

Depreciation can also impose long-term corporate restrictions. With your real estate having an increasingly reduced tax basis, any future sale for a value above the tax basis will trigger gains resulting in your eventual tax payment. With highly depreciated real estate, the tax consequences from a sale can be material, potentially compelling you to seek restrictive strategies that will continue to allow you to defer the tax payments. Or you may simply discover that the tax consequences are so high that you are better off retaining the real estate. In seeking to avoid the ultimate payment of tax, you are liable to find that you have effectively created your own opportunity cost.

3. **Ability to reset the capital stack.** This pertains to the ability to refinance the asset to revert to the 70% leverage so that equity rates of return do not depress over time as the loan is repaid. As to the issue of diminished equity rates of return associated with changes in OPM and equity mix, there is not a permanence to these changes. Debt can be refinanced and the mix of OPM and equity can potentially revert to its original level. However, there are often material costs associated with constant balance sheet refinancing, and most fixed rate borrowings on commercial real estate come with prepayment costs and restrictions.

A discussion of loan prepayment restrictions leads to the examination of important qualitative features that can make a material difference to your business. For instance, if loans cannot be easily prepaid, then a decline in your OPM mix can mean that your equity in the real estate is effectively beyond reach; it is trapped. Likewise, if you undertake fixed-rate loans that have prepayment restrictions, and if such loans are not assumable, then selling or recapitalizing your business could be more challenging.

Over many years of providing real estate capital to middle market and larger companies, I have witnessed the destructive impact that poor financing decisions can have on wealth creation.

The preceding lease-versus-own case study goes a long way toward explaining why we founded STORE Capital to provide real estate lease solutions to nonrated, bank dependent companies. Real estate capital stack options that permit companies to readily own their commercial real estate are generally not that exciting. However, markets change over time, which demands that OPM capital providers likewise change. For users of OPM, the lesson is simple: Constant OPM shopping and evaluation can reward you with elevated capital efficiency and corporate financial flexibility. Both can contribute highly to EMVA creation.

Real Estate as an Investment

While it is hard for growing companies to efficiently own their real estate today, there are a number of success stories of companies that prospered through real estate ownership. The most notable example is chain restaurant industry leader McDonald's, which early on decided to own its real estate and the real estate operated by its franchisees. At the time, Ray Kroc, the empresario who bought McDonald's and then grew it to the world's largest fast-food chain, was not primarily thinking of the potential of real estate as an investment. He was concerned with being able to exert higher levels of control over his franchise community.[1] In the early years of McDonald's and the chain restaurant industry, it was common for franchisees to deviate from mandated practices and even menu items. Real estate ownership gave McDonald's an added important tool to compel franchisee compliance beyond the franchise agreement. By the end of 2019, McDonald's was among the largest real estate companies in the world, closing in on nearly $40 billion of real estate investments. McDonald's stands nearly alone among the major franchised restaurant chains in its ability to execute a strategy centered in real estate ownership.

Another success story I enjoy is that of Discount Tire, a company based a few miles from STORE Capital's office. This impressive business was started in 1960 by Bruce Halle with just $400. In 1970 he moved from Ann Arbor, Michigan, to Scottsdale, Arizona. At that time, the company had just seven locations. Ultimately, Bruce and his team grew the company to become the nation's largest independent tire and wheel retailer, with over 1,000 stores across the county. By the time of Bruce Halle's death in 2018, he was the wealthiest person in Arizona and included in the Forbes 400 list of richest Americans, with an estimated net worth of $6 billion.

The original Discount Tire store in Ann Arbor, Michigan
Credit: Discount Tire

A key part of Bruce's strategy over the years was real estate ownership. This was accomplished in part by not ordering real estate financing solutions off a traditional menu. Instead, Discount Tire often received attractive real estate financing from a novel source: the tire companies that supplied the business. As I noted at the beginning of this chapter, real estate ownership will always be the first choice, providing the advance rate is high enough, the payments are low enough, and corporate flexibility is not impaired. Unlike McDonald's, Discount Tire realized its profound success as a privately held company, with real estate ownership facilitated through such innovative strategies.

One final key observation to be made about real estate ownership is that it's fundamentally an investment activity. The election to own real estate can be expected to entail a materially higher equity commitment than the option to lease. In essence, a company electing to own real estate is getting into the same business as STORE Capital, whereas a company leasing from STORE Capital is deciding to use its equity rather than their own. STORE has a reliable business model capable of delivering consistent returns over time, but with returns that can pale beside the potent business models and growth engines belonging to its many tenants. STORE's customers would generally prefer to have the company commit its equity to their real estate while they preserve their own equity to accelerate their growth using their more potent business models. They would rather have a landlord than a banker who can provide only part of the real estate capital they need.

At a certain point, companies can become so successful and generate so much cash flow that they are happy investing their cash flow into real estate. Bruce Halle and his financial team at Discount Tire knew about our companies, and we would have welcomed the chance to count them as a customer. But they simply did not need the money. Their business model was so potent and their financing strategy so well-conceived that they were able to expand beyond the ownership of an operating company to also become successful real estate investors.

Chapter 9
Opportunity Cost

One of the great books in business is *Economics in One Lesson* by Henry Hazlitt. First published in 1946, he wrote it when he served as the principal editorial writer on finance and economics for *The New York Times*. The first chapter in this book is entitled "The Broken Window," where he describes the economics of a broken shop window, together with the thoughts that often accompany such an event. For example, you might say that, while a nuisance, the broken window simultaneously creates a societal opportunity. A job will be created to replace the window and the income earned by the associated labor force will then benefit others as the money they earn flows through the economy. Such thoughts are commonplace as we consider the repercussions of accidents or natural disasters. In making such observations, our tendency is to think about what *is* and what we can *see*.

Henry Hazlitt

In this case, the window is broken.

But what about what *could have been?* Had the window *not* been broken, the shopkeeper could have taken the money needed to replace the window and spent it elsewhere, benefiting other businesses. In turn, that same money would have flowed through the economy to create new jobs and perhaps build new buildings, rather than just repair existing ones. But that opportunity was lost, with the resultant cost of the broken window.

Instead, the shopkeeper had to spend money just to stay even; from his expenditure he realized no additional benefit or value.

Think of this as an opportunity cost.

Companies incur opportunity costs like this every day. The groundwork for these costs is laid by leadership that, like Hazlitt's window example, is focused on what *is*, rather than what *might be*. Often, opportunity costs arise from capital stack and OPM choices.

This chapter is designed to offer an illustrative framework to help assess the impact of opportunity cost probability and thereby help you capture *future opportunity value.*

Some Opportunity Cost Illustrations

Consider this example. You are offered an attractive loan to finance the purchase of a piece of real estate used in your business. The advance rate is aggressive, the interest rate is amongst the best you have seen, and you can live with the financial covenants. But what happens if you want to change your business model in a way that creates a risk of covenant violation? Or what happens if you elect to sell the building, or your business and the loan is not assumable or desirable? Or what happens if you want to pay off or modify the loan, only to discover that modifications are difficult and expensive and that there is a material prepayment penalty? Like our earlier window illustration, these are "what ifs," whereas business leaders all too often focus on the "what is."

Here is another illustration. Let's say that you learn about, and consider, an alternate means of OPM for your building. You choose to sell it and then to rent it back in what is called a sale-leaseback arrangement. You like the real estate price and the lease rate offered by your proposed landlord, and you accept the deal. But sometime later, you elect to sell your company and you find that the lease is not assumable without landlord consent, which exposes you to business risk, elevated legal bills, and extended time.

Or maybe you one day find that the property is such a strong performer that you would like to expand it. You go to the landlord to see if they can help fund the expansion. They can't, or won't, and it turns out that borrowing for the expansion is hard because there is no way to pledge the expansion of another person's real estate to your bank.

The opposite could also happen. You find that the property is not performing well, and you would like to close it down or relocate it, so you ask your landlord for help. Again, the landlord takes a pass. Your landlord likes this location and prefers you to pay the rent obligation, even it means that you will suffer meaningful losses. Maybe your landlord financed the real estate in such a way as to impose financial flexibility limitations that would disallow location closure, lease assignment, or an asset substitution. Oftentimes, financial limitations imposed on landlords by *their* lenders become *your* financial limitations.

In both the preceding real estate OPM illustrations, one pertaining to mortgage loan financing and the other pertaining to a landlord lease arrangement, the business leader focused on what *is* rather than what *might be*. In so doing, both real estate OPM solutions imposed potential long-term corporate opportunity costs. The business leader, by locking in favorable financing while at the same time ignoring the possibilities for resultant corporate constraints, set in motion this opportunity cost potential. Or, looking at the glass half full: The business leader made it difficult or impossible to harvest opportunity value that could have been there. Leaving opportunity value on the table can cost a great deal.

A big reason business leaders fall prey to opportunity costs is because *opportunity value capture* is hypothetical, whereas the financing terms delivered by various OPM choices are known. We are brought up to think this way, hearing maxims such as "a bird in the hand is worth two in the bush," and so are generally conditioned to overlook hypotheticals. Should future problems arise from our capital stack or operational decisions, we simply assume we can readily address them later.

Creating a Model to Evaluate Real Estate Lease Opportunity Costs

Part of the problem in evaluating opportunity costs is knowing how to begin to estimate the opportunity value we are giving up. I will start our opportunity cost case study by evaluating the impact to your business of being partners with an intractable real estate landlord. This is purely illustrative. The important elements to be taken away from this chapter pertain to how to set up the problem as you quantify the potential costs of lost opportunity value.

Invariably, multilocation retail and service companies have some locations that do not pencil out. For our initial illustration, assume that 5% of your locations underperform. To evaluate the impact on your business, we will use the restaurant case study and wealth creation illustration from chapter 4:

Restaurant Case Study

1 Business Investment		$1,000,000
2 Sales		1,500,000
3 Operating Profit (EBITDAR)	Profit margin is 20% of revenues	300,000
4 Maintenance CapEx	2% of business investment annually	20,000
5 OPM	OPM is 75% of business investment	750,000
6 Interest and Rent Expense	Cost of OPM is 9%	67,500
7 Pre-Tax Cash Flow	3 - 4 - 6	212,500
8 After-Tax Cash Flow	75% of cash flow	159,375
9 Equity	Opposite of OPM (25% of business investment)	250,000
Return on Equity		
Pre-Tax	7 ÷ 9	85.0%
After-Tax	8 ÷ 9	63.8%

. . . and the resultant all-important Wealth Creation Formulas:

Equity Valuation Multiple: Your Current Equity Rate of Return
÷ Required Investor Equity Return
or
$$85\% \div 20\% = 4.25X$$

Equity Value: The Amount of Original Equity Invested
× Equity Valuation Multiple
or
$$\$250,000 \times 4.25 = \$1,062,500$$

EMVA Creation: The Amount of Equity Invested
× (Equity Valuation Multiple − 1)
or
$$\$250,000 \times 3.25 = \$812,500$$

In our illustration, your business has an operating profit margin of 20%. But if just 5% of your properties post reduced operating profit margins of 10% each, then this would drag your EBITDAR margin down by .5%, which is computed by multiplying the 10% profit drag by the 5% of properties underperforming. In total, your operating profit margin would be reduced from 20% to 19.5%.

I might say that this is a mild description of the possible.

It is not uncommon for underperforming assets to have no operating profit margins at all, in which case the 5% of the properties might have a comparative profit drag of 20%. That would reduce your overall EBITDAR margin by 1% (that is, 5% × 20%). And if 10% of your assets underperform, that would lower your EBITDAR margin by a full 2% (10% × 20%). I have seen companies that have had far greater challenges, facing larger percentages of underperforming locations having negative operating profit margins. Here's a draconian case: 20% of your locations underperform, swinging from a 20% operating margin *profit* to a 20% operating margin *loss*. The unfortunate result: An 8% change in your operating profit margin, from 20% to 12% (20% of locations × a 40% operating margin drag). Faced with such dismal results from those locations, you would likely want to go to your landlords to see what you might be able to do to offset this profit drag. There could be the potential to improve the properties in such a way as to help recover lost profitability. Or you might seek to sublease, close, or relocate those locations.

Unfortunately for you, it is not uncommon for landlords to decline your requests. They frequently view their business arrangement with you as having been carved in stone the day you signed your lease. And it is not uncommon for landlords to offer no money to aid with improvements to your underperforming properties. Or perhaps they have restrictions imposed on them by their lenders that become *your* restrictions.

Landlords are often intractable, which can exact a material cost. You are often on your own.

During my years of providing real estate capital solutions to businesses, I have heard many stories of such landlords. Often, those stories can shape the views of business leaders, leading them away from landlord solutions and toward banker solutions. Not infrequently, I have listened to the chief financial officers of real estate–intensive companies expound on the essentiality of owning their mission-critical real estate.

To this, I would note that commercial real estate lenders often deliver products having material restrictions of their own. These can range from covenants to modification, prepayment, and assignability constraints. Moreover, because real estate ownership invariably requires an elevated mix of equity, corporate returns and value creation can be adversely impacted, and the capital stack can be harder to adjust. A key part of the reason for ultimate capital stack adjustment inflexibility is often that real estate owned for a long time becomes characterized by an increasingly low tax basis as a result of accumulated depreciation. In such cases, even if the real estate is sold for its original cost, the taxable gains can be enormous, often precluding using lease OPM at a future date. This is a big reason why some well-established and larger companies continue to own their real estate; the tax consequences of real estate divestitures can make altering their capital stacks in favor of leasing alternatives too costly.

To the problems imposed by leasing poorly performing properties from intractable landlords, there is a flip side: You could have *outperforming* properties that you would like to expand, and yet you're saddled with intractable landlords. Let's say that you have 5% of your properties that outperform, and you would like to expand them. The cost for the expansion will be 25% of the initial cost of the property, but the added revenues will be 10%. Best of all, the incremental operating profit margin from the revenues will be 40%, reflective of the high margins you can generate on your marginal (or last dollar of) revenues after all your fixed costs are covered.

This set of circumstances will impact four of your six V-Formula Variables.

The first variable to be impacted is sales, which is computed by multiplying the percent of outperforming locations to be expanded by the 10% in expected same store sales growth. In this first illustration the sales growth amount to .5% (5% × 10%).

The second variable is the operating profit margin change, which works out like this:

% of outperforming stores

×

% of sales increase to be had by expansion

×

% of marginal operating profit margin

or

5% × 10% × 40%

or

.05 × .1 × .4 = .002, or .2%

Five percent of your properties with 10% sales increases each at a 40% margin will raise your overall EBITDAR margin from 20% to 20.2%. If 10% of the stores outperform, your margin increase would be .4%. And if the marginal sales increase is 25% at each remodeled location, your margin increase would rise a full 1%, elevating your overall operating profit margin to 21%. You could be more fortunate and have 20% of your locations outperform, with remodeled and expanded locations seeing 50% increases in revenues. Now your operating profit margin has the potential to improve a full 4%.

Your only problem is that you need your landlord to commit to the 25% expansion dollars, for which you are willing to pay a corresponding increase in your rents. This added business investment is the third V-Formula variable change.

If you are fortunate and your landlord funds the added business investment for you, your OPM mix will rise slightly, which is the final V-Formula variable change. The basic formula for the OPM increase is illustrated as follows:

% of outperforming stores

×

% of increase in business investment required at each location

or

$5\% \times 25\%$

or

$.05 \times .25 = .0125$, or a 1.25% rise in business investment funded with OPM

In this case, if the landlord is funding the expansion of 5% of your locations, the OPM mix rises 1.25%, reducing your equity mix by a like amount and serving to slightly elevate your returns. In the original restaurant example, there is 25% equity committed to support your business investment. Subsequent to the expansion of outperforming locations funded by your landlords, the mix now becomes 76.25% OPM and 23.75% equity.

Landlord commitments to expansion funding is ideal. Unfortunately, many landlords will refuse requests for additional investment. As with the earlier intractable landlord illustration of underperforming properties, you are on your own.

Being on your own is not a good thing when it comes to improving rented real estate. With an inability to pledge the real estate improvements you need to make, the expansion of rented properties will often rely heavily on equity, which will reduce the desirability of rented property expansion and lower corporate equity returns.

While the illustrations of the potential impacts on your company from underperforming or outperforming locations are hypothetical, they reflect a range of possibilities that are not at all far-fetched. So, the question becomes, if you have constraints that limit your ability to address underperforming or outperforming company locations over time, how much can this impact your business value?

When it comes to the potential for underperforming locations, we'll start with the most draconian scenario, with 20% of underperforming locations coupled with a 40% operating profit margin swing from a 20% *profit* to a 20% *loss*. The resultant 8% decline in corporate operating profit margin to 12% causes your current equity rate of return to drop from 85% to 37% representing a nearly 57% of your equity valuation (37% ÷ 85% − 1).

The drop in business valuation arising from operating underperforming locations assumes that you continue to keep those locations open and operational. The key is to find solutions that will either enable a performance reversal or a way to cut your losses. Often, as the well-known investment adage goes, "Your first loss is your best loss."

Here is where it is helpful to have factored into your business model average maintenance capex variable the expected average annual losses of business investment value associated with location closures. Those costs could be in the form of lease termination fees paid to accommodating landlords or simply losses over location cost upon the sale of owned facilities. In the near term, a clear option is often to simply close the facility, rather than incur negative operating profit margins. Given the meaningful 57% loss in equity valuation resulting from open unprofitable locations, there are likely many options that would serve to lessen the adverse corporate impact.

Let's return to outperforming assets. In this case, we will select the optimistic outlier case offered earlier that you can remodel 20% of your locations, with each location to realize a 50% rise in revenues and a 40% profit margin on your incremental sales with an incremental landlord-funded location investment of 25%. Your overall increase in sales amounts to 20% of the locations multiplied by the 50% rise in remodeled store revenues, for a 10% rise in company revenues. The increased margin is computed by multiplying the 20% of locations by the 50% revenue increase by the 40% operating profit margin on marginal sales ($.2 \times .5 \times .4 = .04$, or 4%). Your business investment rises by .5% (20% of the locations multiplied by a 25% rise in location business investment). Finally, your OPM rises by 5% to 80% (20% of the locations multiplied by the 25% rise in remodeled location OPM), resulting in an equivalent drop in relative equity contribution.

With four of the six V-Formula variables impacted by the above illustration, we can use the shortened V-Formula formula construct set forth in Chapter 5. In this case the sales ÷ business investment ratio rises from 1.5:1 to 1.57:1, given the 10% rise in sales and the 5% increase in business investment. The result of the expansion and remodeling effort is a spectacular 67% rise in current pre-tax ROE from 85% to 142%. In turn, the elevated performance raises the equity valuation multiple from 4.25X to 7.1X. This raises your EMVA creation from 3.25X your initial equity invested to 6.1X, or better than $1.5 million.

Case Study V-Formula
20% Location Expansion Case

$$((1.5 \times 1.1) \div (1 \times 1.05) \times 24\% - 80\% \times 9\% - 2\%) \div 20\%$$

Or

$$(1.57 \times 24\% - 80\% \times 9\% - 2\%) \div 20\% = 142\%$$

Equity Valuation Multiple = 143% ÷ 20%, or 7.1X

Equity Value = 7.1 × \$250,000, or \$1,775,000

EMVA Creation = 6.1 × \$250,000, or \$1,550,000

You never know where opportunity costs might bite you. As you know by now, I like to create data tables that illustrate the impacts of changes in V-Formula variables. The table that follows illustrates what can happen to your equity value given different changes in operating margin and equity mix within our restaurant case study. In essence, the table comprises our prior illustrations of the impacts of outperforming and underperforming locations and their impact on your business.

Operating Margin & Capital Stack Equity Valuation Multiplier Impact

				Change in Operating Margin		Potential expandable asset value impact range	
		−8.00%	−4.00%	−2.00%	1.00%	2.00%	4.00%
Change in % Funded with Equity	−5.00%	−48.2%	−12.9%	4.7%	40.6%	49.4%	67.1%
	−2.50%	−52.8%	−21.4%	−5.8%	27.2%	31.9%	47.6%
	−0.50%	−55.8%	−27.0%	−12.6%	12.2%	19.4%	33.8%
	0.00%	−56.5%	−28.2%	−14.1%	7.1%	14.1%	28.2%
	0.50%	−57.1%	−29.4%	−15.6%	8.3%	15.2%	29.1%
	2.50%	−59.5%	−33.8%	−21.0%	4.6%	11.0%	23.8%
	5.00%	−62.0%	−38.4%	−26.7%	0.4%	6.3%	18.0%

Potential underperforming asset value impact range

Limited upside to YOM funded leased asset expansion

Our initial restaurant case study was for a single location having $1.5 million in revenues. Illustrations of the potential impact on your business value of location outperformance or underperformance clearly require a much larger company. It does not matter. Part of the beauty of the V-Formula is that it's all about the interrelationship of the Six Variables.

A few observations on the sensitivity table. Drops in your corporate operating profit margin, taken alone, will have no impact on your equity mix, which is why I put a border around the three squares having no equity alteration for the illustration of underperforming location impact. On the other hand, expanding outperforming properties can be expected to come with an equity mix alteration, which is why I put a border around the nine squares at the top and bottom of the table.

Should you be able to prevail on your various landlords to fund the cost of expansion, and should you be able to limit your corresponding equity investment, then the result could well be a favorable change in your capital stack that results in elevated equity returns. This is reflected at the top right of the table.

On the other hand, the opposite is also true. Should your landlords be intractable, compelling you to make the investment in expansion yourself due to an inability to obtain bank financing on real estate you do not own, then the resultant lower returns from equity funded renovations may cause you to forego your expansion plans.

The equity valuation impact, demonstrated by the lower right-hand squares, of having to fund location expansion with equity is far less compelling. You may simply have a better use for the equity, which means that your landlords will have imposed a permanent cost on your company because of their unwillingness to help you take advantage of your expansion opportunities.

The equity valuation impacts to your business can perhaps be best illustrated pictorially. In this case, the range is simply the top four lines of the data table, since they are most likely and cover the ranges in the bottom right quadrant as well. I basically omitted the bottom left quadrant. Your equity mix can indeed increase if your profit margins fall, but this is not a given; it is at your option.

As you look at the graphic that follows, the most obvious observation is the wide range of opportunity cost outcomes that can swing your equity valuation by nearly 60% or more in either direction.

For fun, I inserted one more variable into the graphic illustration. What if the cost to get a more flexible loan or the cost to have a landlord offering your company added flexibility was an increase in OPM cost from 9% to 9.5%? When introducing the V-Formula and then later discussing the financial efficiency levers at your disposal to improve corporate value, I made the observation that three variables (sales, business investment, and operating profit margin) tend to have an outsized impact on equity rates of return. Behind them would be the capital stack and the OPM/Equity mix. The cost of OPM tends to be the least important variable with respect to business valuation creation. In this case, the half point in excess interest rate serves to reduce your equity valuation by 1.8%, but it provides valuable insurance that enables you to seize inevitable chances to take advantage of opportunity value capture. The likelihood that the higher interest rate would not pay for itself over time is low and represents an intelligent form of opportunity value capture insurance.

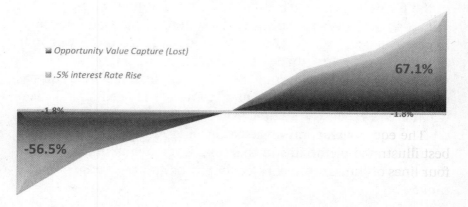

**Opportunity Value-Opportunity Cost Range
Impact on Equity Valuation**

When I first moved to Arizona in 1986, our chairman was Robert Halliday. Bob gained a reputation for his strategic business acumen as the treasurer and director of Boise Cascade, which he helped grow into one of the nation's largest timber and real estate companies. He later became a consummate entrepreneur, helping start a wide range of companies, including Franchise Finance Corporation of America, where I worked.

Bob had cut his leadership teeth decades earlier, serving in the U.S. infantry in northern Africa, then being among the first ashore during the D-Day invasion, and ultimately concluding his service approaching the Rhine River near Aachen, Germany. In total, he received seven Purple Hearts, the last of which was a severe head injury that sent him home for an extensive recuperation.

With all Bob's intellect and collective experience came abundant wisdom. He was among the first people with whom I shared my early V-Formula observations in 1999. Appropriately, one of Bob's most frequent aphorisms was this observation: "Availability of capital is everything." That observation plays out in the preceding illustration. OPM may occasionally be expensive, but it's valuable if it permits continued accretive growth. OPM that lessens your likelihood of corporate opportunity cost imposition is undeniably preferable. Finally, your chances for corporate opportunity value capture tend to be greater with more liquidity. Such liquidity can be in the form of excess cash balances or unused lines of credit. The former will elevate your business investment and the latter involves larger lender commitments, both of which can modestly lower your current pre-tax return on equity.

Over 30 years of working with three successful public companies, we have adhered to Bob's maxim. We have raised capital, even when it was expensive, so long as we were able to deploy the capital in a manner that was accretive. We have likewise added to our liquidity as a way to provide our companies greater margins for error while raising our chances to seize opportunities that came our way.

Chapter 10
The Final Form of OPM

aron Krause founded and owned a small company that manufactured buffer pads. In 2008 he sold the company to 3M, the large Minneapolis-based publicly traded company. At the time of the sale, he retained ownership of one product, a polymer sponge that he had developed to tackle hard cleaning projects. Because the sponge was similar to other products owned by 3M, the company declined to include it in the company purchase.

They would come to regret that decision.

Sometime later, Aaron brought a few of the sponges into his kitchen to use for cleaning dishes, and an idea was born: An effective sponge in the shape of a smiley face, with functional holes representing the eyes and mouth that could be used to aid in the cleaning process. The sponge was cute, easy to clean, and possessed properties that enabled it to become soft in hot water and hard in cold water. In May 2012, Aaron founded a company to manufacture and sell the sponges, which he called Scrub Daddy. In October of that year, Aaron and his idea were invited to the nationally syndicated reality business show *Shark Tank* to make a pitch for an equity investment to the panel of successful entrepreneurs. Aaron was ultimately able to sell 25% of Scrub Daddy to QVC shopping network empresario Lori Greiner for $200,000, valuing the equity of his company, which had minimal revenues, at an even $800,000. A day later, Lori and Aaron sold 42,000 Scrub Daddy sponges on QVC, and they were on their way. That was just the start; over the next two years, they would sell two million units on QVC.[1] Eventually, the product would become available at Walmart, Bed Bath & Beyond, and other national retailers. Through the end of 2019, with cumulative sales surpassing $270 million, the company had expanded into an 80,000-square-foot manufacturing facility producing a line of 20 diverse products capitalizing on the Scrub Daddy name. Not surprisingly, Scrub Daddy secured the title as the best-selling product ever to be presented on *Shark Tank*.

Aaron Krause, founder of Scrub Daddy

"Every day, we're taking market share from 3M," Aaron told *CEO Magazine*. "I know they're kicking themselves for taking Scrub Daddy out of the deal all those years ago."

OPM Equity

Most entrepreneurs start off with limited financial means. Like Aaron Krause, they have an idea for a product. Better still, they may have coalesced an experienced leadership team and conceived a business model. However, to execute the idea requires equity. Short on the YOM (your own money) form of equity that we have used until now, equity is required from other investors. Essentially, this is the final form of OPM: OPM equity.

In the case of Aaron, he was able to obtain $200,000 from Lori Greiner and maintain control of his business. He gave Lori just 25% of the company, convincing her that the business potential for a product having minimal material revenues was well worth her investment. For her part, Lori bought a lot to the table. She had her own successful show on the QVC shopping network, *Clever & Unique Creations,* and had created hundreds of products, many of which she had patented. The pairing of Aaron with Lori was both fortuitous and financially successful for both of them.

How does one convince an investor to part with their money to help you start or grow your own business? More than that, how does one raise OPM equity and give up the least amount of corporate ownership possible? Doing so generally requires harnessing an idea for a product or service to a business model capable of delivering returns likely to exceed typical investor requirements. Convinced that this is possible, independent investors will be willing to make a minority investment (an investment not giving them ultimate corporate control) in your company, leaving you with a majority ownership stake, even though you may have invested little or no YOM in the business. This is how most business leaders create their companies. And if those companies are highly scalable and can grow with minimal new investor equity, the opportunity for personal founder wealth creation simply gets bigger.

I have played a role in the founding of two real estate investment trusts, both of which would go on to be publicly listed on the New York Stock Exchange. Like Aaron, at the time we started our companies, we had minimal revenues and assets. Like Aaron, we made use of OPM equity, which we attracted by pitching our ideas to investors. In our case, we offered corporate presentations together with financial models of our business plans that illustrated our potential to deliver equity returns exceeding minimum investor thresholds. Given our large equity needs, we individually ended up owning a small portion of the businesses we created. Fortunately, those businesses addressed big markets and became large.

Generally, the choice when starting a business comes down to this: You can individually own a big piece of a small pie or a small piece of a big pie. If you can own a big piece of a big pie, as many in the Forbes 400 list of richest Americans have done, then you are, in business terms, a definite unicorn.

Sustainable Growth Rate

One tried and true means of maintaining a high level of corporate ownership is to start a business with YOM and then subsequently sell stakes in a proven business model. Sometimes, YOM may include supportive investment help from friends and family having faith in your ability. To illustrate this, I will return to the simple restaurant case study that we have used throughout this book.

Restaurant Case Study

1 Business Investment		$1,000,000
2 Sales		1,500,000
3 Operating Profit (EBITDAR)	Profit margin is 20% of revenues	300,000
4 Maintenance CapEx	2% of business investment annually	20,000
5 OPM	OPM is 75% of business investment	750,000
6 Interest and Rent Expense	Cost of OPM is 9%	67,500
7 Pre-Tax Cash Flow	3 - 4 - 6	212,500
8 After-Tax Cash Flow	75% of cash flow	159,375
9 Equity	Opposite of OPM (25% of business investment)	250,000
Return on Equity		
Pre-Tax	7 ÷ 9	85.0%
After-Tax	8 ÷ 9	63.8%

. . . **and the resultant all-important Wealth Creation Formulas:**

Equity Valuation Multiple: Your Current Equity Rate of Return
÷ Required Investor Equity Return
or
$$85\% \div 20\% = 4.25X$$

Equity Value: The Amount of Original Equity Invested
× Equity Valuation Multiple
or
$$\$250,000 \times 4.25 = \$1,062,500$$

EMVA Creation: The Amount of Equity Invested
× (Equity Valuation Multiple − 1)
or
$$\$250,000 \times 3.25 = \$812,500$$

In the model, you are generating $212,500 of annual current pre-tax cash flow. Assuming you pay taxes on this amount, you are left with $159,375. Let's say you decide you would like to build a second location, but you have no more YOM with which to make the $250,000 requisite equity investment. All you have is the $159,375 in corporate after-tax cash flow, which represents an after-tax rate of return on your $250,000 equity investment of 63.75%. Remember from our earlier discussions that your personal compensation for running the company is included in the company's operating costs and reflected in the 20% operating profit margin.

Here is an important observation: It turns out that the after-tax rate of return also approximates the *sustainable growth rate*. That is, assuming you could reinvest your $159,375 back into the company, and assuming relative business investment and other V-Formula relationships remain unchanged, you could grow revenues and cash flow by 63.75%.

The precise computation of the sustainable growth rate requires the use of the OPM payment constant, rather than the OPM interest/lease rate in order to arrive at a current free cash flow after-tax return on equity. Hypothetically, if the principal portion of annual OPM repayment were to be 2%, then the payment constant would rise to 11% from the V-Formula interest rate input of 9%, lowering the after-tax current cash equity return (and sustainable growth rate) to 59.25% from 63.75%.

For the purpose of our illustration, I will assume that there is no principal payment, meaning that the after-tax current equity return and the sustainable growth rate are the same. A 63.75% sustainable growth rate analysis might be relevant for many businesses, but less so for a single store restaurant operator. That is because you cannot build 63.75% of your second restaurant. You need to build the whole restaurant!

Taking on OPM Equity

You need $250,000 in equity to contribute to the development of your second restaurant, but you only have $159,375 after-tax cash in the bank from your first year of operations. You are short $90,625, or 36.25% of the equity you require. Since you are doubling the size of your company, you will need a total of $500,000 in equity, of which 18.1% will have to come from OPM equity ($90,625 ÷ $500,000).

The question is, how much of the company will you have to give to your new minority shareholders?

The answer: Approximately 4.26%, which is computed by dividing the portion of equity you need (18.1%) by 4.25 (your equity valuation multiple).

Owning 95.74% of your company (100% – 4.26%) while only personally investing 81.9% of the equity dollars (100% – 18.1%) will increase your personal rates of return. How much will your equity rate of return be on the portion of the business you own?

Current Equity Rate of Return When You Don't Own the Entire Company

Your Company's Current Equity Rate of Return

×

Your Ownership%

÷

Your % of Equity Investment

or

85% × 95.75% ÷ 81.9%

or

.85 × .9575 ÷ .819 = .9937, or 99.37%

Your current pre-tax equity rate of return has now increased from 85% to nearly 100% annually by selling shares in your company to OPM equity investors whose return requirements are less than a quarter of what your company could generate on the equity at cost. With that elevated rate of return, your equity valuation multiple on your portion of company ownership has now risen to about 5X from 4.25X, which is significant. Your new equity investment at cost is $409,395 (your original $250,000, plus the $159,375 in current after-tax cash flow you have reinvested in the business). Altogether, assuming the second location's performance is equivalent to the first, your investment is now worth approximately $2,046,875 ($409,375 × 5). And you have doubled your equity market value added from $812,500 to $1,637,500 (just take your investment of $409,375 and multiply it by 4, which is your equity valuation multiple − 1).

Deciding How Much OPM Equity to Use

The increased valuation from using OPM equity is so impressive that you start to consider the feasibility of raising *all* the money for your second location. In that case, you would be raising 50% of the equity at cost, but only parting with 11.76% of the company ownership (50% ÷ 4.25). Now, your equity rate of return on the $250,000 initial investment rises to a cool 150% annually (85% × 88.4% ÷ 50%). With an annual rate of return of 150% on your $250,000 investment, you would have $375,000 of annual pre-tax cash flow, and your minority shareholders (YOM equity) would have a 20% current pre-tax rate of return on their $250,000 investment, or $50,000. Meanwhile, your equity valuation multiple on your annual pre-tax portion of company cash flow rises to 7.5X (150% ÷ 20%), giving you an equity valuation of $2,812,500 and equity market value added creation of a truly impressive $2,562,500.

Using OPM equity can accelerate your growth and raise your personal wealth. By using OPM equity to fully fund your second restaurant location, your ability to create personal wealth rises by over $1 million. To do this, you had to divest 11.76% of your company's ownership, rather than reinvest your surplus after-tax cash flow and part with 4.26% of the company equity. Keep in mind that your company's sustainable growth rate, assuming all V-Formula variables remain unchanged, is still 63.75%, which is the current after-tax equity return on the aggregate cost of that equity. Only now, the notion of corporate current pre-tax equity returns no longer tells the full story; the equity ownership is unevenly apportioned relative to company cash flows, giving you a 4.25X higher current rate of return than that of your OPM equity. Corporately, the return remains 85% in the aggregate, while your personal actual return will range from 100% to 150%, depending on which of the two OPM equity choices you select. Importantly, however, your sustainable growth rate comes now on a bigger base of two restaurants, giving you the chance to further expand and compound your returns using internally generated cash flows. The initial use of OPM equity helped accelerate this growth and increase your wealth creation potential.

Creating a Five-Year Model

What follows is a five-year illustration of your restaurant business, assuming you part with 11.76% of the company to fully fund the equity needed for your second restaurant location. To keep this really simple, I have assumed that all of the new restaurants are opened the first day of each year, all restaurant variables remain unchanged every year, with no cash flow growth or business model changes at each restaurant from year to year.

	Year 1	Year 2	Year 3	Year 4	Year 5
# Restaurants Built	1	1	2	2	4
Beginning Cash	$0	$159,375	$478,125	$615,625	$1,071,875
YOM	250,000				
OPM Equity		250,000			
Equity Invested in New Locations	(250,000)	(250,000)	(500,000)	(500,000)	(1,000,000)
After-Tax Cash Flow	159,375	318,750	637,500	956,250	1,593,750
Cash Flow Growth Rate		*100.0%*	*100.0%*	*50.0%*	*66.7%*
Ending Cash	$159,375	$478,125	$615,625	$1,071,875	$1,665,625
Company Valuation *(Cash + Equity Value)* *(Assuming after tax current equity return of 15%)*	$1,221,875	$2,603,125	$4,865,625	$7,446,875	$12,290,625
% of Your Ownership	100.00%	88.24%	88.24%	88.24%	88.24%
YOM Current After-Tax Return	63.75%	72.00%	83.72%	68.35%	67.67%
OPM Equity Current After-Tax Return		15.00%	26.09%	31.03%	39.47%

Total Equity Value		$10,625,000
Your Value	88.24%	$9,375,000
OPM Equity Value	11.76%	$1,250,000
Equity at Cost		$4,165,625
Equity Market Value Added		$6,459,375

In the above illustration, you start your company with $250,000 of YOM at the beginning of your first year and quickly open that restaurant. At the start of the second year, you open another location funded with OPM equity. Thereafter, you open another eight restaurants from your free after-tax cash flow, ending your fifth year in business with a company having nearly $1.6 million in free annual cash flow and over $1.6 million of cash in the bank.

You unleash the potency of your business model by compounding your returns through the reinvestment of your free cash flows.

Assuming that a likeminded investor still is looking for a 20% pre-tax cash return, or a 15% after-tax rate of return, $1,593,750 in fifth year after-tax annual cash flow would have a market valuation of $10,625,000 ($1,593,750 in after-tax cash flow divided by .15). In addition, you are sitting on $1,643,750 in cash, which is positioned to be reinvested in the company in year 6 to help continue its impressive growth. Your 88.24% share has a value of $9,375,000, or more than 37 times your initial investment of $250,000, which made all this possible. Altogether, the equity at cost amounts to $4,165,625, which is the sum of the initial YOM and OPM equity investments totaling $500,000 plus two numbers: your reinvested new location equity over five years and your ending cash balance of $1,665,625.

A few other thoughts about the model. First, the V-Formula variables change because the company's cash balances rise every year. Cash balances are effectively another form of business investment and serve to lower your current pre-tax equity rates of return. This is why your annual after-tax rate of return in year 2 falls short of 112.5% (or the 150% pre-tax rate of return less the 25% in taxes). Thereafter, your current equity rates of return gradually fall further as cash balances rise and the free cash flow kept in the business is reinvested at a lower current after-tax rate of return of 63.75%. Conversely, the OPM equity rate of return starts off at the targeted after-tax rate of return of 15% and gradually rises from there. That is because you sold off 11.76% of a one-store operation at a 20% pre-tax and 15% current after-tax rate of return, but then reinvest the OPM equity free cash flows in a business capable of producing a higher current annual after-tax rate of return of 63.75%. This illustrates the value to investors of getting in on the ground floor of an opportunity as corporate free cash flow is reinvested in a growing business, contributing to EMVA creation for all company shareholders.

By the end of year 5, the impressive results have made you a millionaire many times over. Your OPM equity partner is likewise happy, having multiplied the initial investment by nearly six times over a four-year period.

What is your annual compound rate of return on your investment? With no after-tax distributions from the company made for five years and the cash flow reinvested into the company's ten-unit restaurant development plan, the returns are impressive. Your compound after tax annual rate of return amounts to 100% annually on your initial $250,000 investment. That rate of return is a composite of your reinvested after-tax cash flows and your terminal value at the conclusion of the fifth year using a 15% current after-tax return threshold expectation.

I like to break down where investor returns come from. In this case, about 60% of your compound annual rate of return is derived from the reinvested business cash flows, and about 40% of your compound annual rate of return comes from the eventual valuation pop you receive by selling your company to an investor having a lower 15% after-tax threshold (20% pre-tax).

As for the compound annual rate of return on the OPM equity, it, too, is impressive. The OPM equity partner invested in a one-unit restaurant company and then watched you grow the company tenfold. That growth and the reinvestment of OPM equity cash flows caused the compound annual rate of return to be materially above the initial 15% after-tax rate of return threshold, approximating 43%. In so doing, some of the EMVA your business created fell on the OPM equity as its portion of cash flow was reinvested, realizing compound growth in a business capable of delivering a current 85% pre-tax return on equity.

Sweetening the Deal

An important observation to be made from this simple model is that, by constructing only one restaurant in the second year with OPM equity, you end up sitting on cash balances of $159,375 generated in your first year, which effectively lowers your investment yield. However, were you to get a bank line of credit to bridge the remaining amount of the $250,000 you need, you might be able to construct a third location in your second year. Such a credit facility might be available to you, given a company supported by $500,000 in equity, together with a proven business model. With access to such a borrowing facility, it would be a simple matter to model out the development of 15 restaurants over a five-year period.

You might also be able to sweeten your deal. Rather than offer up 11.76% of the company to OPM equity based on your first-year results, you might be able to convince the OPM equity to take less corporate ownership based on your forward cash flow expectations. Those expectations might include the second restaurant to be built with the added equity or even a third restaurant to be built using a bank credit facility. In so doing, you might be able to raise your equity valuation multiple from 4.25X to more than 6X and thereby give away less than 8% of the business for 50% of its contributed cash equity.

Is this kind of personal wealth creation really possible? I have certainly laid out a rosy scenario having solid business model fundamentals, no speedbumps, and with every restaurant location working perfectly and identically. In reality, perfection is elusive. This is especially so in service industries, like restaurants, which require high staffing levels combined with high levels of customer interaction. However, what is clear is that our business model has a meaningful margin for error, which is important.

Apart from these observations, I would anecdotally say that I have seen any number of our customers over the years create extraordinary value in the businesses they have developed and grown. As a provider of real estate capital, playing a small role in their successes has been personally gratifying. Having been a part of starting companies myself, I have likewise benefited personally from such enterprises. Indeed, solid business models executed by great leadership teams, together with return compounding, can literally create wealth from thin air, which is essentially what EMVA is. What is more, powerful business models, implemented and compounded by talented leadership teams, can create material wealth within comparatively brief periods of time.

There is one final important potential sweetener. You started your restaurant enterprise with a single location having modest growth potential. Then OPM equity, together with the compounding from free cash flow reinvestment, enabled you to both diversify your investment holdings and substantially elevate your free cash flow growth rate. An expected benefit of these business model improvements would be a reduction in investor pre-tax current return expectations from 20% to a potentially much lower amount. The result: a potentially far higher equity valuation multiple and resultant EMVA creation.

OPM Equity Flavors

OPM equity comes in various flavors. In our brief five-year case study, OPM equity accepts a minority stake in a company, with the equity investment subject to the same risks and relative voting rights as the initial YOM equity. However, oftentimes, there is little to no YOM equity available to start a company. And, even if there is YOM equity, OPM equity investors may seek some form of investment protection. They are happy to help you financially succeed and achieve wealth, but they do not want to take the same level of personal investment risk. A common solution is to offer OPM equity investors a preferred rate of return, often called a "pref." How much do you have to offer? There are no set guidelines, but investor expectations will be shaped by their investment alternatives at any given time. I have commonly seen annual preferred rates of pre-tax investor returns targeted in the 7% to 10% area.

Typically, companies will have the option to pay annual distributions or to simply accrue the return preference. To draw on our earlier illustration, such an arrangement might mean that the OPM equity would agree to invest $250,000 for an 11.76% stake in your company, subject to achieving a preferred 8% compound annual rate of return as a floor. The risk to you as the initial company shareholder is that, if 11.76% of company pre-tax cash flow falls below 8% of the OPM equity investment, the OPM equity will then lay claim to a larger portion of the business equity cash flows and corresponding value.

With an OPM equity preferred rate of return, there is effectively what is called a *cash flow waterfall*. First, the OPM equity realizes their pre-tax 8% compound annual rate of return. Second, you realize your pre-tax 8% compound annual rate of return on your percent of equity ownership. Then the remaining cash flow is divided between you and the OPM equity relative to your respective company ownership percentages. Given that you have issued equity for 11.76% of the company based on a 20% current annual pre-tax rate of return, your margin of error is large. With OPM equity that allows you to double your company's size, you could suffer a 60% drop in current pre-tax cash flow ((8% pre-tax preferred rate of return ÷ 20% pre-tax equity valuation capitalization rate) – 1) before your OPM equity would realize less than an 8% rate of return resulting in your share of annual cash flow falling below your 88.25% equity ownership. As you cross the 60% drop in cash flow barrier, you cede higher portions of cash flow to your OPM partner. However, given that you provided the first half of the equity, your sensitivity to reduced cash flow is less. Even if your operating cash flow falls 90% short, your equity partner receives just over 47% of the corporate cash flow to realize the 8% return preference.

What if you are lacking funds to even start that first restaurant location? In such a case, raising OPM equity will be more challenging and will almost certainly demand a preferred rate of return. Assuming for a moment that you could raise the full $250,000 for your first location and assuming that you could convince your OPM shareholders to accept 23.53% of the company (100% of the equity divided by your 4.25X equity valuation multiple), with a preferred rate of return of 8%, your margin for error would still be a 60% deviation in cash flow from predicted levels. However, performance deviations will have twice the impact of the results derived from raising half the cash equity and parting with 11.76% of the company. At a 90% deviation, your OPM equity partner is entitled to more than 94% of the corporate cash flows.

Starting a company using OPM and OPM equity could put you on the path to achieving Mort's Model. The key lays in having a meaningful margin of error.

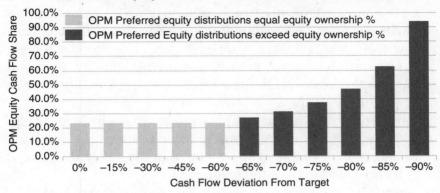

OPM Equity Considerations

Most companies are started by entrepreneurs having little in the way of YOM, making reliance on OPM equity commonplace. Here, just as with OPM, it pays to shop. In fact, OPM equity characteristics and arrangements can vary greatly. OPM equity approaches to investment and management can vary as well. Likewise, finding the right cultural and personality fits with your fellow equity holders is extremely important. Beyond these important considerations, I have made three key OPM equity observations over the years:

1. **Buy-sell arrangements.** When relying on OPM equity, it is always wise to incorporate an ability to one day buy out your OPM equity investors. If their target rate of return is 20%, perhaps you can have a written agreement to buy your OPM equity out at five times cash flow (which equates to a 20% pre-tax yield) beyond a certain date. Your OPM equity investors would likely also expect a return preference on a buyout. Generally, OPM equity is open to a sale arrangement because minority investors tend to be interested in understanding eventual exit strategies. For you, having a purchase option adds greatly to your personal corporate flexibility.

2. **Corporate organization chart simplicity.** Do your best to keep your corporate organization chart simple. Over the years, I have watched as entrepreneurs have issued OPM equity in

multiple companies they have created. For instance, I have seen restaurant operators place each location into a separate company having separate ownership. In one such instance, the company eventually went public, but not before enduring months of OPM equity negotiations for each of the various entities. That was because the founders also failed to follow the above advice with respect to OPM equity purchase options.

Keeping your corporate organization chart simple also helps with financiers. You are far more likely to have access to bank financing with financial statements that are easily understood and encompass your entire operation.

3. **Maintain majority ownership.** To paraphrase my long-time business partner Mort Fleischer, owning 51% of a company is almost as good as owning 100%, since you are indisputably in charge. Such a focus on control can importance be likewise seen in the over 200 public companies that have multiple classes of stock. Examples include such names as Berkshire Hathaway, Alphabet, and Facebook. Among the first public American companies to adopt this approach was Ford Motor Company, whose Class B shares were initially created 1935 to provide 100% voting control. Later, upon the company's 1956 initial public offering, the terms were altered to limit the Ford family descendants to just 40% of the voting rights, together with a corporate liquidation preference. All this despite the Class B shares representing a fraction of the company's equity value.

Chapter 11
A Look at Public Companies

On August 19, 2004, approximately nine years after its founding, Google launched its initial public offering (IPO), selling 22.5 million shares (about 7% of diluted equity), netting the company over $1.9 billion. The company hardly needed the money. Google had long transformed its idea for a superior internet search engine into a potent business model, and at the time of its IPO was sitting on nearly $550 million in cash and no debt.

By the end of that year, the company's cash hoard had grown to $2.1 billion. A year later, the company would have over $8 billion in cash and the cash balances would grow uninterrupted from there. By the end of 2019, the company was sitting on a pile of nearly $120 billion in cash and was debt-free.

If you are wondering why Google felt the need to go public, it wasn't for the money. It was for the enhanced corporate valuation and for the liquidity offered to employees and founding shareholders, including Larry Page, Sergey Brin, and various sophisticated private and institutional early investors. Between the company's IPO and the end of 2019, the two original founders would each divest more than $10 billion in shares and yet still retain stock valued at more than $25 billion each. Given that they hold class B shares that provide them with 10 share votes for every share of stock they hold, at the end of 2019, Larry and Sergey controlled over 51% of the voting power of the company. By that time, the company they founded had also become the fourth to ever reach $1 trillion in market value. Cumulatively, Google (later folded into a holding company named Alphabet) had created an astounding $689 billion in equity market value added, helping propel many of its early shareholders and employees into the ranks of the ultra-wealthy.

During the 15 years between its 2004 public offering and the end of 2019, Google had no need to use the public markets to issue added shares of stock. Meanwhile revenues climbed at nearly a 35% compound annual rate from almost $1.5 billion at the end of 2003 to over $160 billion in 2019. During that period, Google would materially grow its initial internet search engine franchise. At the same time, the company aggressively expanded through corporate acquisitions, purchasing over 230 companies engaged in diverse technology-centric business activities. Some of the company's biggest acquisitions included Motorola Mobility, YouTube, Double-Click, Nest Labs, and Fitbit. Given Google's expansion into diverse products ranging from self-driving cars to computer manufacture, video sharing, web-based television, cell phone operating systems, home automation, and wearable technology, the company elected to change the name of the public company to Alphabet in 2015, reflecting its status as a diverse technology holding company. Still, over 80% of the company's 2019 revenues and most of its profits were derived from advertising activity associated with its internet search endeavors, with many of the new technological initiatives having limited near-term financial success. The company's most notable failure came with its largest single acquisition: the $13 billion buyout of Motorola Mobility, which it sold to Lenovo two years later for just $2.9 billion, though it retained much of the investment's intellectual property. All this change and product exploration was telegraphed to investors upon the company's IPO in an iconic letter from Sergey and Larry in which they noted they had no intention of ever being a conventional company. Indeed, they have not been a conventional company, which means that their business model is subject to constant change from the potent, simple model they originally brought to the table in their 2004 IPO.

Another name for a holding company that owns a variety of independent, free-standing, unrelated businesses is a "conglomerate." Such companies can be difficult for analysts and investors to decipher because their financial statements tend to provide limited financial disclosure by business line.

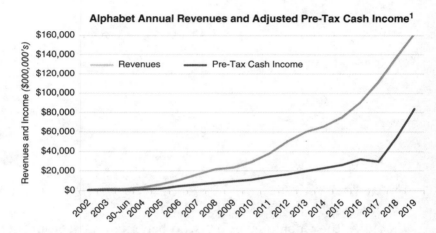

¹Pre-tax income before non-recurring costs, depreciation, amortization, and non-cash compensation.

Over two decades of uninterrupted revenue and income growth, Alphabet impressively maintained an after-tax current equity return consistently in the area of 20%. What is really notable is that, by 2019, slightly over half of the business investment in the company consisted of cash, which was just sitting on the balance sheet. Were excess cash to have been returned to shareholders, after-tax current equity returns from year to year would have generally doubled, or occasionally tripled. There was a fair amount of current return volatility from year to year, but for Alphabet to achieve this kind of performance while realizing outsized compound growth was a rare accomplishment. All the more impressive is that the company achieved this kind of performance while absorbing more than 230 acquisitions. With that said, were one to have access to detailed business line performance, it would not be surprising to see highly divergent underlying current equity returns.

The following chart shows Google's sustained current after-tax equity returns since its IPO. Given the company's large cash balances, which elevate business investment and lower equity returns, I also elected to illustrate even more impressive returns eliminating the company's excess cash balances.

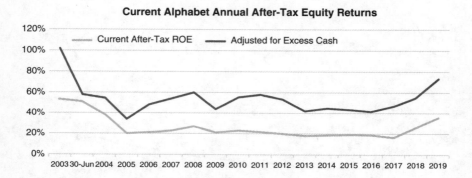

Current Alphabet Annual After-Tax Equity Returns

Of course, the Google investors who benefited most from the company's impressive annual current equity returns and return compounding were the original shareholders. This is because they enjoyed a material markup of their investment in publicly listing the company, serving to depress the comparative returns of subsequent shareholders. In recalling the earlier case study of the restaurant company used throughout this book, the current pre-tax equity return sought by third-party investors having similar risk and growth expectations was 20% annually. But the public markets can be generous, especially when they see outsized potential for growth. For 2004, Google's pre-tax equity rate of return approximated 46%. By the end of the year, barely six months following its IPO, Google's shares had nearly doubled in value, approaching a price of $200. Computing current equity rates of return using such a share price would yield an approximate current equity pre-tax rate of just 2%, or far lower than the 20% in our case study.

Google's equity valuation multiple exceeded 20X. However, at the time, Google investors were willing to make this bet, which centered on the earnings growth potential of its internet search franchise, together with further earnings growth expectations driven by the reinvestment of their small portion of the company's growing free cash flow at far higher pre-tax rates of return. They would be rewarded for their confidence.

In the previous chapter, I provided a case study example of a restaurant operator doubling the equity investment in the company using OPM equity while retaining over 88% of the ownership. Issuing shares to investors at unequal valuations means that a corporate current equity return no longer tells the whole story. In the case of Google, the $1.9 billion raised from its IPO represented close to two thirds of the company's equity at cost, while ceding just around 7% of company ownership. Corporate current equity returns do provide insight into the quality of a corporate business model, but they don't tell you much about how the returns are divided. With the share dilution from the Google's IPO, the current equity returns in 2004 for the founding shareholders were in the ballpark of 20X the current returns accorded to the new public equity holders.

With the equity investment relative to cost divided unequally from the outset, all equity holders would then proportionally benefit from Google's stellar future performance based on their ownership, with the shares multiplying in value by about 50 times between the IPO and the end of 2019. Not coincidentally, revenues likewise rose by about 50-fold.

Investors making the early bet to invest in Google were highly rewarded with returns well in excess of those realized by the broader stock market. In buying in at the IPO and having their 7% ownership of current equity returns reinvested in the company at its elevated rates of return, they participated in a like amount of future EMVA creation. Some of the wealth created from thin air would fall on them. Between Google's IPO and the end of 2010, investor returns approached 28% annually, trouncing broader stock performance indices.

Of course, as companies grow, "the denominator effect" starts to kick in, which is to say that as the company gets larger, it becomes more difficult to sustain outsized growth. In that vein, between 2010 and 2019, Google's revenues increased far less, growing 5.5 times, which was still impressive. Were you to have invested in Google's shares in 2010, the value of those shares would have risen about 4.6 times over that nine-year period, providing a compound annual rate of return of approximately 16%. While that figure represented strong performance, outperforming the roughly 14% annual return from the broader stock market (using the S&P 500 Index), this is still far from the results realized by the earliest public shareholders and light years from the returns realized by the company's founding shareholders, whose collective basis in the company's stock at cost was about 5% of that of the IPO investors.

When talking about a company like Alphabet, grouping the founding shareholders together does not tell the complete story. This is because the equity divisions between the company's founders, Sergey Brin and Larry Page, and early important shareholders, would not have been based on the cost basis of their respective equity contributions. Key early shareholders who helped to seed Google included Andy Bechtolsheim, founder of Sun Microsystems; Ram Shriram, a former executive with Netscape, an early internet search engine provider; David Cheriton, a Stanford computer science professor and serial technology entrepreneur; Jeffery Bezos, founder of Amazon; Eric Schmidt, who would serve as president of the company from 2001 to 2011 and then later as executive chairman; and John Doerr of the venture capital company Kleiner Perkins, who would also go on to serve as a board member of Alphabet. All these early shareholders would go on to be worth billions of dollars each from Google and other investments, with Jeff Bezos eventually rising to the top of the Forbes' 400 list of wealthiest Americans and claiming the title as the world's richest person. However, when it comes to Google, the division of equity value ultimately benefited the two initial founders the most. As graduate students at the time of the company's conceptualization, Sergey and Larry would ultimately be dependent on OPM equity, likely having little or no cost basis in their shares of the company, and ultimately serving as shining examples of the possibilities of realizing Mort's Model.

Determining Public Stock Equity Returns

The approach introduced in this book to computing current equity rates of return can be modified for stock market investors. Determining current corporate equity returns and the quality of a corporate business model using the V-Formula is informative but falls short of what it means to evaluate a company like Alphabet as a personal stock investment.

To do this requires that you compute Alphabet's EMVA and involves three steps:

1. **Compute the equity market capitalization of the company.** The absolute easiest way is to use the company's equity market capitalization available from virtually any online stock quotation provider. Or you can look to a company's public quarterly (10-Q) or annual (10-K) Securities and Exchange Commission (SEC) filings to see the share count, which is typically in small type somewhere at the bottom of the first page. You can always get a link to corporate SEC filings from the website of any public company, or you can go directly to the SEC itself, which has a search engine called "Edgar." To compute the company's equity market capitalization, simply multiply the number of shares by the daily stock price.

2. **Compute the cost of Alphabet's equity.** To do this, I look at the financial statements of the company, adding the cost of the cash assets of a company and subtracting from this cost the cash obligations, or liabilities. I ignore such balance sheet items as accumulated depreciation, together with non-cash accounting conventions, such as "right to use" assets or liabilities or straight-lined rents.

3. Compute Alphabet's EMVA as follows:

Equity Market Capitalization – Company Equity at Cost = EMVA

To determine equity returns available to shareholders requires various V-Formula adjustments using EMVA. This is because a current shareholder cannot buy Alphabet at cost. The company has been marked up and the amount of that markup is equal to EMVA. This means that business investment, from the viewpoint of a shareholder, cannot be simply computed from the company point of view. EMVA added or lost must be incorporated into the equation as follows:

Public Shareholder Business Investment

Hard Asset Variables

(Land, Building, Furniture, Fixtures and Equipment You Buy &
Land Building, Furniture, Fixtures and Equipment You Could Buy, but Rent

& Working Capital Variables

+ (Accounts Receivable, Inventory, Cash Balances, Prepaid & Deferred Costs)
−(Accounts Payable, Accrued Expenses, Deferred Income, Deposits & Other 0 – Cost Liabilities))

& EMVA

Chances are that you may not be able to figure out the rents on "Land, building, furniture, fixtures and equipment you could buy, but rent instead." If you can't figure this out, it's all right. The V-Formula will still compute current equity rates of return. On the other hand, if you have an idea how much reported rent expense is for items that might otherwise have been owned, then "capitalize" the rent expense into business investment as follows:

Adjusting Reported OPM for Assets Leased Rather Than Owned

Lease Expense ÷ Predicted Market Lease Rate = Estimated Value of Leased Assets
(Add the estimated value of leased assets to both business investment and OPM.)

I prefer to take this approach whenever I can to make companies more comparable. Oftentimes, the differences between the balance sheets of two companies can be whittled down to who rents and who owns their hard assets. As a result, capitalizing the assets of companies that elect to rent their hard assets can give much better insight into their comparable use of OPM, as well as a better understanding of the estimated cost of assets they deploy in their business. Keep in mind that you will be adding the computed value of leased assets to both the business investment and *also* to the amount of OPM used. At the same time, you will need to back out of corporate operating expenses the rents for these assets, which will serve to elevate the company's operating profit margin variable.

If you are unable to make an estimate of the value of leased assets that could otherwise have been bought, then your operating profit margin will be lower, as will your business investment and OPM, but the V-Formula result will be the same.

Earlier I noted that business investment cannot generally be readily determined from accountant-prepared financial statements. Part of this is due to the noise created by non-cash accounting conventions. Part of this is also because accounting rules permit companies to alter their hard asset investment amounts. For instance, if I decide to sell a piece of real estate I own at a loss, accountants will expect me to "impair" the asset and literally mark its cost down to estimated market value. Or, if I am Google and need to take a $10.1 billion write-down on my business investment in Motorola Mobility, then either hard assets or intangible assets (goodwill) might be so impacted. Of course, from a finance point of view, none of this alters the business investment made or the fact that the current equity rate of return is less because of a few problem investments—in this case, real estate, or the business value of an acquisition. By eliminating or lowering the value of assets, the accounting profession impedes our ability to precisely know what the actual business investment was. Therefore, this elimination of corporate business investment costs prevents us from completely understanding how much EMVA company leadership has added to or taken away from the business. What's more, the financial disclosure associated with asset valuation write-downs will typically seek to minimize their importance by noting them to be "non-cash." This is not true. The investments clearly consumed cash and were a part of business investment, but that cash was simply invested in a prior period. Again, this is where finance and accounting can diverge, with the latter obscuring the image of the former. From a financial vantage point, you cannot alter business investment with non-cash adjustments like depreciation or impairments.

Presuming equity market value added to be a positive number (and not all public companies trade for values worth more than their equity at cost), then incorporating it into the V-Formula will lower the computed current pre-tax and after-tax equity rates of return, often by a lot. For one thing, the ratio of sales to business investment will be a great deal lower. In the case of Google's 2004 year-end financial statements, the ratio falls from 1.05:1 at business investment cost to just .06:1 with EMVA added to that cost. If your company makes use of OPM, then your OPM mix will also be lower, which will further lower your comparable equity rate of return. The one small positive will be that your maintenance capex, staying constant as a number, will be less as a percentage or your new elevated business investment number.

Making such adjustments to the V-Formula inputs to compute current corporate equity returns transforms the V-Formula. Now, the formula no longer computes current corporate equity rates of return at cost; instead, it computes the current returns realized by the public shareholders. I refer to this revised value equation as the Market V-Formula.

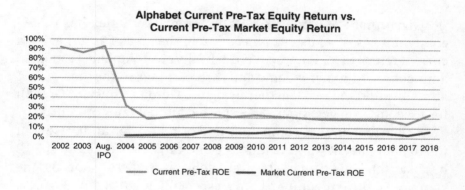

So, how does the market equity return of Alphabet stack up to the earlier current equity return graph? For one thing, it will be a bit more volatile. This is because EMVA is subject to the normal volatility of a company's business model and also to the volatility delivered by the changing sentiments of public markets. Between 2004 and 2019, Alphabet's after-tax market return on equity averaged 5%. Adjust this amount for the excess cash, and the average current after-tax equity return available for shareholders investing in Alphabet shares would rise to nearly 7%.

**Alphabet Current Market After-Tax Equity Returns
with Cash Earnings Growth**

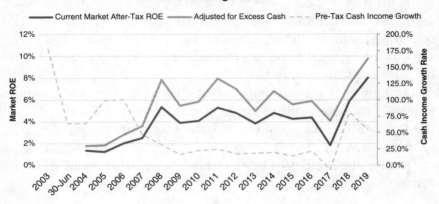

Given that the broad S&P 500 stock market index has posted equity returns since its 1926 inception in the area of 10%, having a current return of 5% is attractive, especially given Alphabet's median annual growth in net income and cash earnings in the area of 23% annually. Add the two together using the Gordan Constant Growth formula and you get about 28% expected annual rates of return.

The actual annual compound rate of return for an investment in Alphabet in 2004 and held to the end of 2019 was closer to 20% because the public markets ultimately placed less value on the company's current equity returns, especially in 2018 and 2019. As companies age, outsized growth becomes harder to maintain, and so share valuations tend to decline relative to equity cash flows. In other words, the price of shares and the EMVA created did not rise as fast as cash flow growth.

A current after-tax market equity return is interesting, but Alphabet did not pay any of that cash flow out to its shareholders in the form of dividends. Instead, it retained and reinvested all its cash flow into the business. Therefore, an investor at the end of 2019, electing to make an investment in Alphabet shares, would be electing to buy into an 8% current market equity return with the hope that such a return could grow through the compounding available through cash flow reinvestment as well as cash flow growth from its various businesses. Was that a good deal? For sure, the rate of growth in cash income experienced a fair amount of volatility between 2017 and 2019, suggesting less predictability. However, by historic valuations and historic rates of growth, the price of Alphabet shares at the end of 2019 would appear to have been historically attractive. And, indeed, the company delivered shareholder returns of over 30% over the following 12 months, or more than double the returns delivered by the broad S&P 500 index.

Walmart

Companies and their business models change over time. At the same time Alphabet was delivering growth powered by a consistently strong corporate business model, Walmart, the largest retail chain in the United States, was on a different path. Founded in 1962 by Sam Walton, the first Walmart store in Rogers, Arkansas, redefined retailing by eliminating middlemen and selling merchandise at consistently low prices. Fifty-eight years later, by the end of its fiscal year ending January 31 2020, Walmart had expanded globally, employing over 1.5 million and serving as the largest employer in 22 states. The company also had an equity market capitalization of nearly $325 billion, of which $121 billion was equity market value added. EMVA as a percentage of equity at cost approximated 40%. At the end of 2019, the Forbes 400 list of wealthiest Americans included no fewer than seven members of the Walton family, boasting combined estimated net worths exceeding $200 billion. As impressive as this is, the Walmart business model was not as robust as it had been in its earlier years. The company had become a mature business operating within a less hospitable, highly competitive marketplace.

For its fiscal year ended January 31, 2000, Walmart posted a current pre-tax equity return of approximately 25%, not materially different from the returns posted by Alphabet, though with a capital stack composed of approximately 44% of OPM. The portion of OPM is hardly a surprise; Walmart is not an asset-light company, operating many thousands of costly locations with multiple banners across the globe.

Incidentally, Walmart is a good example of a company that elects to lease a fair amount of its real estate assets that it might otherwise own. Between January 2000 and January 2020, company rent expense rose from $573 million to over $3 billion annually. Using estimated rental capitalization rates of 7% in 2000 and 6% in 2020, the estimated value of leased real estate OPM proceeds would rise from approximately $8 billion in 2000 to approximately $60 billion in 2020.

By contrast, Alphabet had historically been operated with little or no OPM, which is unusually low for a public company and adversely impacts equity returns in comparison to a business like Walmart.

By end the company's 2020 fiscal year, Walmart's current pre-tax equity rate of return had fallen to below 15%, driven by some operating profit margin compression and even more by a decline in its ratio of sales to business investment, from around 2.5:1 to roughly 1.7:1.

Over 20 years, Walmart's business model changes resulted in lower current equity returns and EMVA erosion. Between its fiscal years ending January 31, 2001, and January 31, 2020, Walmart actually lost nearly $145 billion in EMVA as follows:

($000,000s) Walmart Equity Market Value Added Change	FY 2001 – FY 2020
Cash Flow from Operations	$437,954
Less: Stock Repurchased	(107,795)
Less: Dividends Paid	(86,864)
Equals Equity Cash Reinvested In Business	$243,295
Less: Actual Increase in Equity Market Valuation	(98,509)
Equals Market Value Lost	$144,786

In the 20 years between fiscal years 2001 and 2020, Walmart generated over $435 billion in cash, using $108 billion to repurchase approximately 37% of the company's shares and another $87 billion to pay dividends, leaving $243 billion of its realized cash flows over that period in the company. Assuming that equity sum was reinvested into the business, one would expect the company would have raised its equity capitalization by a like amount. In that case, Walmart would have created no EMVA on the reinvested cash; the company's value would simply rise by the equity reinvested in the business. However, the company's equity valuation rose by approximately 40% of the free equity cash flow reinvested in the business, meaning that approximately 60% of the reinvested cash flow effectively evaporated. The result was a loss in EMVA of nearly $145 billion.

This illustrates that a company can metaphorically "light money on fire" in the process of growing its share price and earnings per share. Over the 20-year period from 2001 to 2020, Walmart's share price did slowly grow, eventually more than doubling. As a result, shareholders who held on to their Walmart shares over this entire period realized a comparatively anemic rate of return of less than 6% annually. That included the Walton family, which collectively held approximately half the company's shares at the beginning of 2020. Walmart may have underperformed over 20 years, but the net worths of Walton family members grew from the modest share price appreciation (below 4%, compounded annually), together with the collection of more than $40 billion in dividends.

That the Walton family could slowly and steadily grow their net worths over a 20-year time frame as the company they founded lost EMVA and underperformed the broader stock market is instructive. You can indeed get richer holding onto poorly performing investments, even as they erode EMVA. And investors are often content to earn modest returns as they search for safety. Given Walmart's size, market position, and financial strength, many investors would characterize the company as safe. And, indeed, the company lived up to this expectation, recovering lost EMVA during a global pandemic and delivering shareholders an approximate 25% rate of return for its 2021 fiscal year.

In the 1920s, iconic comedian Groucho Marx invested heavily in the stock market. As all the stock prices rose, it looked like easy money! But in the great stock market crash of 1929, Groucho lost $800,000—his entire net worth. He later joked that he would've lost more, but that was all the money he had.

He and his brothers slowly rebuilt their fortunes. Later, he was asked by a floor trader on the New York Stock Exchange what he invested in. Groucho replied that he invested in Treasury bonds. The trader shouted back that Treasury bonds, historically considered to be the safest of investments, don't make much money. "They do," Groucho retorted, "if you have enough of them."

If you are an equity investor thinking about investing in Walmart, what might this history tell you?

First off, it would say that Walmart's business model is no longer the same lucrative one that created an ocean of wealth out of thin air for shareholders and the Walton family. Over the 20-year period between 2001 and 2020, EMVA as a multiple of equity at cost fell from approximately 4.3X to less than .6X.[1]

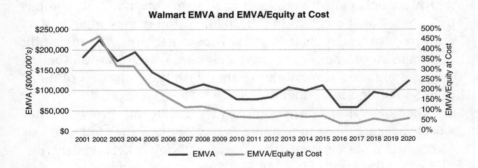

Second, it would say that a substantial portion of the company's retained after-tax current market equity return (or the amount of cash flow kept in the company after the payment of dividends) is subject to evaporation as the company invests its free retained cash flow into lower yielding investments. Indeed, time and changing market dynamics contributed to Walmart's transformation from an EMVA-creating machine to a company that *destroyed* value in the process of delivering modest investor returns.

As an important rule of thumb, one would be selective about being a "buy and hold" investor in a company having business model limitations. Instead, when investing in a large company having a propensity for destroying the value of much of its free retained cash flows, one would generally consider their equity price entry point and then target an exit point. By contrast, holding onto shares in companies like Alphabet, which have steady business models capable of EMVA creation, tends to correlate with less long-term performance risk. Above all, a key observation to be made is that companies and their business models change from year to year. Few growth companies can maintain growth and deliver elevated returns forever.

Chapter 12
Animal Spirits

Up to this point, I have painted a highly rational picture of the way businesses are valued and deliver shareholder EMVA. At the heart of this image lies the ability of businesses to reliably deliver current equity returns. But facts have a way of interfering with such an orderly worldview. I can hear you thinking about the heady valuations often accorded public companies possessing little or nothing in the way of operating profit margins, together with business models that have yet to be proven or defined.

In his seminal 1936 work, "The General Theory of Employment, Interest, and Money," British economist John Maynard Keynes pointed out that the world does not work as neatly as mathematical expectations might suggest. Instead, spontaneous optimism and urges to action arising from "animal spirits" can cause actual market performance to

John Maynard Keynes

deviate from what might be expected. Nearly a century later, the prevalent influence of social media could only serve to magnify animal spirit formation. Keynes's observations would place him at the forefront of the eventual study of behavioral economics.

Public companies, of which there were fewer than 4,000 in the United States at the end of 2020, are often different with respect to the immediate linkage between corporate business models and equity valuations.[1] Occasionally, investor sentiment, the ability to easily trade, and the resultant elevated corporate capital access have the potential to cause the relationship to blur.

Between 1995 and 2000, the Nasdaq Composite stock market index rose 400%, ultimately reaching a mindboggling price–earnings ratio of 200. The dot-com bubble, named for the many overly hyped public companies engaged in the cyberspace race to harness new internet product delivery technologies, left many investors bleeding. Between March 2000 and October 2002, under the weight of a sea of business failures and earnings disappointments, the Nasdaq Composite stock market index fell 78%, wiping out all the gains from the bubble.

Just 10 years prior, the Nikkei 225 Index of leading Japanese companies rode a similar hype-driven wave, reaching an all-time high of almost 39,000 and an untenable price-earnings ratio of 80. The peak of the Japanese stock market occurred at approximately the same time as the fall of the Berlin Wall, which would ultimately lead to the unification of East and West Germany. At the height of the Japanese stock bubble, the value of Nippon Telegraph and Telephone alone exceeded the combined value of all West German–based public companies. Over the next two and half years, the Nikkei index would, like the Nasdaq index a decade later, lose over 75% of its value. By the end of 2020, the Nikkei 225 Index was still approximately 30% short of its all-time high.

While the Nasdaq Composite Index was on its way to its eventual dot-com supernova, I was president of Franchise Finance Corporation of America (FFCA), a New York Stock Exchange–listed real estate investment trust. REITs have historically provided stable rates of return, generally offering far less volatility than might be found in growth stocks and certainly less volatility than in the heady Nasdaq-listed shares in the late 1990s. On an investor visit in New York, Mort Fleischer and I called on Tiger Funds, which was led by Julian Robertson. At the time, Tiger had realized outsized growth and performance, becoming the second largest hedge fund in the world. We were asked what kind of investor rates of return we believed we could deliver, and I responded that I thought we could offer returns in the area of 10% to 12% annually, with most of that being delivered in the form of dividends. The Tiger portfolio manager was unimpressed. "We are looking to make 10% *a month*," he said. And then, considering FFCA a bit more, suggested that our stock was simply part of the "value clutter" to be found among less interesting companies.

It turned out that had you held FFCA from the time of our 1994 IPO until our eventual August 2001 sale to GE Capital, your compound annual rate of return would have been just north of 12%. By then, Julian Robertson had shut down the Tiger Funds following bad bets on currencies and against heady Nasdaq technology shares that had diminished his historically impressive performance. That last bet, had his funds stayed open, would have eventually proved to have been right.

Stock market and asset valuation bubbles are not unusual. They have occurred throughout history. In 2000, I had an opportunity to listen to legendary investor Warren Buffett speak. At the time, his company, Berkshire Hathaway, had avoided placing any bets on the stocks of companies having strategies centered on emerging internet technologies. When asked about the reason for his avoidance of such investments, Warren produced two slides highlighting companies that pioneered two other life-changing twentieth century technologies: automobiles and air travel. There were so many public airlines and automobile manufacturers, most lost to history, that the names of the companies were barely recognizable to the audience. (Ever hear of automobile companies named Doble, Stanley, Ross, or Stearns? No? They, and many more, manufactured practical, operational steam-powered automobiles at the turn of the century.) With that demonstration, Warren noted that, had you elected to invest money in all these emerging companies, you would not have generated any return. Selecting the ultimate winners would have been beyond the skills of most investors. More than this, the ultimate corporate winners from groundbreaking technologies were often not just pioneering manufacturers, but other industries. Oil companies and hospitality are just two of the industries whose growth was kick-started by innovations in transportation technology. Warren preferred instead to invest with a clear understanding of the corporate business models employed by the companies whose stocks he and his company owned.

Elon Musk and Tesla

Quite often, money simply chases stocks based on confidence in the potential of new technologies and the market disruptors who harness them. On June 10, 2010, Tesla became the first automotive manufacturer to go public in 50 years, proposing to be the leader in emerging electric automotive technology. The company was

guided by charismatic leader Elon Musk, who had dropped out of
a PhD program at Stanford after just two days to engage in a series
of highly successful start-ups in software, online banking, and digital payments. The wealth he created from these ventures enabled
him to be an early investor in Google. He also invested $30 million
in Tesla, later assuming the role of chief executive officer. Over
the 10-year period from 2010 to 2019, Tesla never once had a year
in which it realized operating profitability, racking up over $5 bil-
lion in negative earnings before depreciation, amortization, and
interest expense. The company would fund these collective losses,
together with added business investment, through the issuance of
approximately $6.5 billion in new equity and another $9.9 billion
in borrowings.

During this money-losing stretch, Tesla's well-designed electric
automobiles gained in popularity, helping to significantly drive up
the company's share price. With the company reporting its first
positive annual earnings results in 2020, its shares leapt in value,
propelling the company's equity capitalization to more than $630
billion by the end of the year. At that price, Tesla's shares were
worth about the same as the world's 10 largest auto makers combined. Collectively, those 10 companies produced over 50 million
vehicles in 2019. Tesla's production goal for 2020 approximated just
about 1% of this amount, or 500,000 cars. With an approximate 20%
ownership of Tesla, Elon Musk vaulted into first place amongst the
wealthiest Americans, ahead of Jeff Bezos, the founder and CEO
of Amazon.

Meanwhile, the company's precise eventual business model
remained subject to conjecture, given its history of losses and modest 2020 current equity returns. Clearly investors, as reflected in
Tesla's elevated share price, bought into the dream. Yet while the
company's share valuation relative to other quality automotive participants was suggestive of a bubble, the eventual proof lay in its
developing business model.

Stock Exchange Differences

In the United States, there are two major stock exchanges that are the largest in the world. The oldest of these is the New York Stock Exchange, which traces its roots to 1792. An important element for listing a company on the New York Stock Exchange is the requirement that the business have been profitable for the previous three years. The three public companies I have helped lead and take public have all been listed in the New York Stock Exchange. In 1971, the Nasdaq stock market was founded as the world's first fully electronic stock exchange, with no listing requirement that a company ever had been profitable. This key listing criteria difference led Nasdaq to be the market of choice for unprofitable start-ups that are often technology-based, such as Tesla. Many such ambitious, but unprofitable companies, lay at the center of the dot-com bubble. There is always a risk with newly listed public companies that their business models and, hence, equity rates of return are evolving and not readily knowable. With unprofitable companies, this is especially so, adding a clear venture capital component to what had historically been a marketplace comprised of companies having more proven histories and business models.

What this means is that public and private companies often do not play by the same rules. With the vast majority of companies in the United States, the link between business models, equity returns, and equity value creation is more immediate. However, with publicly traded companies, this linkage can, for a while anyway, be obscured amidst rapidly changing financial data, compounded with elements of sentiment and hype (or animal spirits) that accompany the ease, simplicity, and liquidity of a readily tradable instrument.

How long is a while? It can be a long time. The story of an experienced investor like Julian Robertson can bear this out. His strategy was to simultaneously bet in favor of established "old world" companies, while betting against the overhyped valuations of scarcely profitable technology companies caught up in the dot-com wave. It took far longer than he anticipated for those once-lofty valuations to come down to earth.

Restaurant Case Studies

Throughout this book, I have relied on a simple case study of a restaurant company to lay out the framework of the Six Variables that drive business performance and equity valuation. There are more restaurant locations in the United States than any other consumer-facing business, and any number of restaurant chains have tried their hand at going public. More often than not, such ventures do not end well. Between 2000 and 2019, 41 restaurant chains sold shares to the public. Of these companies, about a third remained public with shares trading above their initial IPO price. About 10% of the companies would eventually be taken private at valuations above their initial share price. Slightly more than 40% of the companies were split between remaining public or being taken private at valuations lower than their IPO price. Finally, about 15% of the restaurant IPOs ultimately sought bankruptcy protection.

A big reason for this variability in performance lies in rapidly changing corporate business models. With little in the way of operating leverage, achieving earnings growth typically requires new restaurant expansion. To maintain the same level of earnings growth each year often requires near geometric expansion to offset same-store operating profitability declines as "honeymoon" revenues taper off at locations opened in recent years. Often, companies incur operational and financial stress associated with managing rapid growth as unimpressive business models become apparent.

Lone Star Steakhouse & Saloon

In 1992, Lone Star Steakhouse & Saloon, based in Wichita, Kansas, went public. A year earlier, the company had just six restaurant locations. By the end of 1992, that number had grown to 32 locations. A year later: 68 locations. In 1993, 1994, and 1995, Lone Star was awarded the distinction of "Best small business in the country" by *Forbes* magazine, and in 1994 it ranked #6 in *Fortune* magazine's list of fastest-growing companies.[2]

A shuttered Lone Star Restaurant in Johnstown, Pennsylvania, 2016

In the course of this rapid growth, the company's business model was scarcely visible. By the end of 1995, the company had issued over $200 million in equity and was sitting on nearly $70 million in cash. The company's equity returns were hampered in part because of the elevated cash balances, which meant that their business investment was excessive. Another factor was that their use of OPM stood at just over 15%, a low percentage for an asset-heavy restaurant operator. However, one way to accelerate earnings growth is to use less OPM, since interest or real estate rent costs would otherwise lower corporate profitability and earnings growth. At the time, Lone Star was trading at a hefty price-earnings multiple of 25X. While net income is not exactly cash, if you invert a price-earnings multiple, you arrive at an income yield of around 4% (1 ÷ 25). At the time, this was materially less than the yields that lenders or landlords would demand on their capital. Hence, the company took advantage of its current cost of equity, issuing another $110 million in stock in 1996. By the end of the year, the company's equity valuation approached $1.4 billion, with more than $850 million of that amount being equity market value added.

The company ended 1996 with 207 locations and over $150 million in cash on its balance sheet. Then, with the weight of elevated competition, continued expansion demands, and the difficulty in maintaining same-store sales levels as their locations matured, the business model suffered and revealed itself. By the end of 1997, the company had grown to 265 locations, but the after-tax equity returns were a less impressive 13%, falling to under 7% in 1998, at which point the company's EMVA turned negative.

A year later, the company's after-tax current equity rate of return stood below 4%, with an equity capitalization valued nearly $380 million below its cost. Given that investors could buy the company shares below their cost to create, their market rate of return approximated 8%. Faced with equity rates of return on its own shares that exceeded the returns available from its corporate business model, Lone Star began to buy back stock, acquiring approximately $150 million worth of shares between 1998 and 2000.

Buying back shares of stock, just like paying dividends, has the impact of lowering company business investment, making the pie smaller. Only with stock buybacks, the selling shareholders get the cash as opposed to all shareholders ratably. The result is that the remaining shareholders will see comparatively higher earnings per share growth, but against the backdrop of a shrinking company. Mathematically, this often tends to have little impact on their expected rates of return. For Lone Star, the share repurchases did little to move the company's share price. By 2001, the company's poor performance caught the attention of an activist shareholder who, with holdings of just 1,100 shares, unseated Lone Star's founding CEO from the board of directors, where he served as chairman.

Ultimately, in August 2009, the company was taken private at a price just north of $27 a share. At the time, the company had reduced its restaurant count to 222 locations. That price turned out to be overly optimistic. Seven years later, the company would be in bankruptcy, with all its Lone Star locations shuttered, save a single independently owned outlet on the island of Guam.

Boston Chicken

About a year after Lone Star went public, a fledgling "fast casual" chain called Boston Chicken was listed on the Nasdaq exchange. Founded in 1985 in Newton, Massachusetts, the chain had expanded rapidly in the 1990s. Driven by the growth of its franchise community, most of whom were financed by the company, Boston Chicken was opening a location per day. To enable this growth, the company became a frequent equity issuer, while also accessing copious amounts of OPM. By early 1997, the company, now renamed Boston Market, had over 1,100 locations, with most of them franchised and collectively generating over $1 billion in revenues.[3] By the end of the year, the company would report a loss of over $200 million on revenues of slightly over $460 million.[4] Unsurprisingly, the company's share price plummeted by more than 82% over the course of 1997. A year later, the losses would accelerate, amounting to over $430 million for the first half of the year. With its liquidity effectively evaporated, the company would file for bankruptcy protection in October. Indeed, all the growth, together with a lack of transparency regarding restaurant location operating results, masked the company's faulty business model. In the end, Boston Market turned out to be mostly a lender having no loss reserves, providing capital to otherwise unfinanceable franchisees who collectively operated massively unprofitable locations that were plagued by excessive business investment demands given the sales amount each location was able to generate.

Less than a year following the Boston Chicken IPO, I was engaged in taking FFCA public. With our net lease portfolio exclusively devoted to restaurants and, given that Boston Chicken was the country's single hottest restaurant concept (often paying top dollar for real estate nationwide), we were frequently asked about our views on the chicken chain. Our comment was that we could not see our way to owning any locations because we did not understand the unit-level economics. The company and its franchisees would not share this data with us, but we suspected that Boston

Chicken's business model was flawed. So did some of our share-holders, who tried in vain to bet against the shares as they rose to loftier levels before ultimately crashing to earth.

Value Investing

In 2013, Eugene Fama, a professor of economics at the University of Chicago, was awarded the Nobel Prize in economics for his work on efficient markets theories. In his influential 1970 review paper, Dr. Fama posited that stock prices reflect all available information. A corollary to the Efficient Markets Hypothesis (EMH) is that it is virtually impossible for the average investor to beat the market. This notion has been widely accepted and has given rise to a proliferation of passive stock market index funds. Memorably, in 2007, Warren Buffett bet $1 million that the S&P 500

Nobel Laureate Eugene Fama
Credit: © Nobel Media AB.
Photo: A. Mahmoud

would beat the 10-year performance of a basket of five hedge funds selected by a firm called Protégé Partners. By the end of 2017, the S&P 500 had gained over 85%, while the hedge fund basket had eked out a mere 22% gain.

While this story again served as evidence that Dr. Fama was correct, it does not mean that all stocks are rightly valued based on their underlying business model fundamentals. "Animal spirits" can create valuation distortions that can last a while. Dr. Fama's observation simply meant that corporate share prices reflect their supply and demand based upon broadly held investor sentiment.

Business model fundamentals ultimately prevail. As a student of business models, I know these to be fundamental to wealth creation. In a famous 2008 letter to his shareholders, Warren Buffett paraphrased his former teacher, Benjamin Graham, saying, "Price is what you pay; value is what you get." And, in being a value investor, Warren has a stated preference to buy "quality merchandise when it is marked down." To my way of thinking, when it comes to stock purchases, this simply means investing in quality companies whose current market equity returns well exceed what might normally be expected by a rational investor.

Like many business leaders, I have experienced the personal disappointment of being marked down. STORE Capital went public in October 2014 at a price of $18.50 a share. From there, the company successfully embarked on our planned path to deliver shareholders annual double-digit rates of return. But in the second half of 2016, investor sentiment turned. Interest rates started to rise along with economic growth expectations as investors began to rotate away from defensive dividend stocks, such as STORE. By the end of 2016, news outlets were rife with speculation regarding large estimates of future retail store closings resulting from potent online competition. While STORE was an acronym for Single Tenant Operational Real Estate, many investors unfamiliar with us simply assumed we had a lot of exposure to retail "stores" on the brink of closure. Given these multiple headwinds, our shares fell 20%, reaching a price of $24 by April 2017. Then, at the beginning of May, our shares declined another 19% to approximately $20 owing to a disappointing earnings call from a peer public company Mort Fleischer and I had co-founded in 2003. Investor sentiment assumed that their problems were also likely to be our problems. Meanwhile, with nearly all the share price gains from our IPO lost, our business model fundamentals remain unchanged. STORE was marked down and delivering a high level of current market equity returns.

Before we took STORE public, I approached Berkshire Hathaway, a renowned value investor led by Warren Buffett, with a business proposition, sending an email to the company's general mailbox. Berkshire declined my proposal but liked our business model and the talented team we had assembled. They continued to follow STORE, reading our press releases, earnings call transcripts, and investor presentations over the years. Benefiting from this research, they were prepared to invest when we were marked down. So, in June 2017, Berkshire approached us to buy 10% of STORE's equity, ultimately acquiring just shy of that a week later through a direct stock sale. Of course, we did not like the share price, but we also knew we could make accretive use of the proceeds from the approximately $375 million stock issuance. Bob Halliday's prescient advice regarding the importance of the availability of capital came to mind. More than this, in the face of an unwarranted selloff in our shares, we added to our roster a noted value investor. Basically, we got what amounted to an overnight "Good Housekeeping" seal of approval in an otherwise chaotic market. Our shares immediately rebounded more than 11% and continued up from there. By the end of 2017, our shareholders benefited from a double-digit rate of return for the year. By November 2019, with our shares approaching $40, the annual return to Berkshire Hathaway for their opportunistic value-driven decision was better than 30% annually.

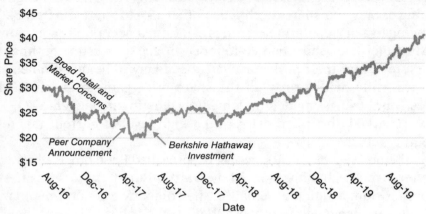

STORE Share Price
Shown from August 2016 to November 2019

Businesses are the driving force of EMVA creation, which is fundamental to our overall economic growth and the essential element that gives rise to the creation of the largest personal fortunes ever assembled. But every so often, companies can be mispriced, resulting in a decline in EMVA and a rise in current market equity returns. This is the fertile ground where value investors seek to play.

I believe business models lie at the vortex of value. Think of a whirlpool in which excessively valued businesses ultimately find their values sucked into the center. They may be able to defy gravity for a while, but business models eventually provide the ultimate valuation litmus test. Now also think of an inverted whirlpool, wherein poorly valued companies ultimately see their valuations get sucked upward. Value investors tend to hover within the inverted whirlpool, trying their best to avoid the animal spirits that often surround companies residing above the vortex of the whirlpool. Interestingly, this is also where private company business leaders tend to congregate. While private companies can be subject to valuation volatility and euphoria, such tends to be far less than with public companies. None of the companies I have been associated with have ever had the luxury of being able to raise capital without an articulated business model. None of our businesses have benefited from overhyped stock prices in a public market. Instead, like most businesspeople, we have had to demonstrate our ability to support OPM, deliver equity returns, and create EMVA.

Overvalued Businesses

**Business Model
Valuation Equilibrium**

Undervalued Businesses

Chapter 13
Mergers and Acquisitions

Mergers and acquisitions (or M&A, as it's referred to among capital markets professionals) refers to the wheeling and dealing that transpires when one company decides to buy another. The acquisition target company can be paid for in outright cash, in which case it is a purchase, or it can be paid for in shares of stock, in which case it is technically a merger of two companies. Either way, one company ends up being the acquiror and the other winds up being acquired. Sometimes, you may hear people talk of a "merger of equals," which suggests a business combination and not really an acquisition. Such events happen, but they are rare and often risky. One of the biggest such events was the 1998 "merger" of automobile manufacturers Chrysler and Daimler-Benz, which was really a $37 billion buyout, and which fell apart in 2007 when Daimler-Benz unceremoniously unloaded its American partner, effectively paying private equity firm Cerberus Capital to take over Chrysler's operations. For its part, Cerberus infused over $7 billion into the company before the company's equity value was effectively wiped out in a bankruptcy filing two years later.

There can be many reasons for a company to grow through business acquisitions. High on the list is operational synergies, which means that you are able to combine another company into your own company and improve your operating profit margin by spreading your relatively fixed operating costs over a larger enterprise. With greater size may also come purchasing efficiencies, whereby you are able to earn greater discounts on the cost of inventory and supplies. Maybe you simply have a better operating model, which can improve the operating profit margin of the company you are acquiring. The company you acquire may be operating in a different geographic market with a different customer base, which allows you to lower your company's operating risk through greater customer diversity. Or perhaps the targeted company sells different products that are complementary to yours, allowing you to be more competitive, possess a more complete business line and be a "one-stop shop."

Whatever the reason, a company's acquisition of another company should enhance its long-term corporate business model and raise its prospects for wealth creation.

Of course, there is one more major reason to buy a company: You are not now in business, but see a business you like, believe in, and believe you can run – and you want to own it. Many businesspeople eventually become business owners not by starting a company but by buying an existing business.

Whether you are the leader of a company contemplating an acquisition or an individual considering a company investment or purchase, one key question is the same: How much should you pay? By now, being versed in current shareholder returns and in the components of building a business, you should have a pretty good idea of how to value a business.

Importantly, buying an existing enterprise means that you are likely to have a clear idea of the business investment required. You will also know the revenues and the operating profit margin, and you will also have an idea of your maintenance capex requirements. So, when it comes to buying a company, the amount and cost of OPM tend to be the two greatest unknowns of the Six Variables. These two variables guide the formation of your capital stack, since the percentage funded with equity, the final piece of the puzzle, is simply the inverse of the percentage of your company purchase price to be funded with OPM.

OPM Capital Options

When it comes to buying an existing business, you'll likely want to craft your own OPM stack from scratch. Your goal in assembling an OPM stack will generally be to start with the longest-term OPM possible having the lowest monthly payment requirements. This order of operations was first discussed in chapter 3, but we will expand on it here.

The name of the game is to keep your *payment constant* (your annual payment on OPM proceeds as a percentage of the OPM proceeds) as low as possible. Drawing on and expanding our earlier discussion, here are some of the many OPM capital options to be considered:

Asset-backed lines of credit (ABLs). These are credit lines, mostly from banks, which are secured by inventory and accounts receivable, with advances and line availability tied to the amount of eligible collateral. These borrowings are generally allowed to be "interest only" because the source of repayment is viewed by lenders to not be free corporate cash flow after interest expense, but the conversion of the assets (inventory and accounts receivable) into cash through the operating cash flow cycle of the company. ABL facilities are appropriate where the proportion of assets centered in accounts receivable or inventory is higher.

Real estate or equipment loans. If the business needs real estate or equipment to operate, then the assets may be financeable over long periods of time, since they tend to be long-lived assets. Lenders may include banks or insurance companies, to name two.

Real estate or equipment leases. For businesses using real estate and equipment, another option is to lease them. This capital solution is where I have personally spent most of my career and is valuable because it's fixed rate, replaces both borrowings and the equity needed to purchase real estate, and has the lowest payment constant you can generally get from OPM.

Term debt secured by assets. This is debt (mostly from banks and other finance companies) having a schedule of repayment over time. The assets pledged can range from furniture, fixtures, and equipment to intellectual property. In many cases, OPM providers will be willing to simply lend based on the recurring cash flow of the business. Often, principal payments start off being very modest and then grow over time with corporate free cash flow.

Other term debt flavors. Occasionally, asset-based credit facilities and term borrowings will be effectively combined into what lenders call "unitranche" borrowings. "Tranche" is a word that comes from old French, literally means "slice," and is used in finance to denote debt demarcations. For instance, over my career, our companies have issued multiple term notes secured by the same assets, with some notes (or tranches) being senior to others and being assigned different credit ratings. In my experience, unitranche lenders often tend to be non-bank finance companies.

Assumed borrowings. There may be some borrowings at the company that are worth assuming. Or perhaps there are borrowings that cannot be prepaid and need to be a part of your capital structure. Prepayment penalties associated with company purchases are not uncommon and represent an added buyer business investment.

Mezzanine borrowing. A "mezzanine" is generally a floor between the first and second in a building, often with a view of the lobby. Likewise, mezzanine debt is also not on the ground floor, with the accompanying first lien position on assets. Mezzanine debt is junior to most other borrowings and often lightly secured with junior asset liens. Sometimes, mezzanine borrowings can be included in a unitranche lending solution. The good news about mezzanine debt is that it is long term. It will tend to be meaningfully more expensive than senior lien borrowings, but often some of the interest payments do not have to be paid in cash; that portion of the interest owed is occasionally "payment in kind," or PIK interest, which means that it is accrued and added to the loan balance.

Seller financing. If sellers are willing to carry back financing, this can be a great way to finance a company because such financing is most often unsecured, generally subordinated to other borrowings, viewed by banks and other sources of capital to be like equity, and often interest-only and long term. Basically, it can be a cheaper and easier form of mezzanine debt.

I should add there may be other sources of such junior or mezzanine capital out there, not the least of which will be friends and family.

Finding the right mix of OPM is not easy. There are numerous sources of capital available that generally depend on company size and type. For instance, asset-backed lines of credit tend to be used for companies having large amounts of inventory and accounts receivable. Such companies can range from FUBU, which we discussed in chapter 2, to automobile dealerships, which obtain asset-based lines of credit called "floorplan" lines to finance their vehicle inventory.

Smaller companies may have access to Small Business Administration (SBA) borrowings. The SBA was set up in by Congress in 1953 to encourage bank loans to fledgling companies. SBA loan programs enable banks to write small business loans while undertaking less risk of loss owing to the government agency loan guarantees that range from 50% to 85% of the principal provided.

There is a veritable alphabet soup of capital suppliers set up to deliver you OPM as you, or the business you lead, seek to buy a company. In truth, putting an optimal capital stack together can be highly creative and may include such elements as preferred stock (non-voting equity that is simply entitled to a defined yield) or debt having ownership conversion rights. Likewise, preferred stock and convertible debt might be redeemable on the option of the OPM issuer or callable (prepaid) upon your option.

Personally, I find all the OPM options to be fascinating. Indeed, the menu of OPM offerings and the list of OPM providers has greatly changed over my career. Conceiving and sourcing the amount of OPM you can prudently use to buy a company is often a puzzle that can take some time to solve.

Solving for Equity and Company Valuation

Once you have determined the amount of OPM you are willing to take on to make a company purchase, you can determine company value and the amount of equity you require. The three steps of solving for equity and company value are simple:

Valuing a Business in Three Steps

1. Determine Pre-Tax Equity Investor Cash Flow:

Operating Profits – Maintenance CapEx – OPM payments

2. Determine Equity Value:

Pre-Tax Equity Investor Cash Flow
  ÷ Required Current Equity Return

3. Determine Company Value:

Equity Value + OPM

You may be wondering how to compute the required equity rate of return. Until now, I have simply said that this is an investor yield that is deemed acceptable, given company risks and growth prospects. Hence, in our often-used restaurant case study, the current pre-tax equity rate of return is 85% for the original investor, while the subsequent investor is happy to achieve a 20% current pre-tax rate of return. There are certainly theories written in business textbooks regarding the determination of expected rates of return. However, my experience is that there is a great variance in the range of corporate business valuations that defy textbook analysis. I have seen people harness Mort's Model and buy companies with virtually nothing down. I have also witnessed business purchasers make substantial equity commitments while chasing after comparatively modest current equity returns. With this being the case, it does not always follow that the amount of equity committed to a company accompanies higher equity valuation.

At our first public company, the biggest private company tenant business failure we encountered was ironically the one having the highest level of shareholder equity commitment.

Sometimes, there are great deals to be had and, other times, not. The law of large numbers, when looked at over a long time, may suggest that there is rhyme and reason to company valuations. I am personally less convinced. There are simply too many elements that can influence company valuations, starting with the motivations of the seller and buyer, and the type and length of the auction process used.

It is rare for company purchase prices to make sense just by maintaining the operational status quo. Ideally, you would like to be able to run a company just as the seller had and realize attractive current equity returns, together with added potential for growth. However, frequently, sellers understand that their companies have the potential for corporate operating efficiency improvements. As a result, sellers often demand elevated prices that drive down current equity returns, compelling corporate efficiency improvements to justify the price paid for the business.

That work generally includes pulling your financial levers, which we described in chapter 7, including:

1. **Improved operating efficiency,** with operating margins enhanced through increased sales, reduced costs, or operational synergies with your existing business.
2. **Improved asset efficiency** realized by shortening the cash flow cycle (assuming an operating model that is more "asset light") or other initiatives to lower the amount of business investment.

3. Improved capital efficiency realized through a more optimal OPM mix or other initiatives designed to lower your comparative cost of capital.

Assuming operational and asset efficiency improvements are to be incorporated in a business purchase, your corporate valuation methodology will often require adjustments by modifying operating profitability and business investment in the first two steps of business valuation shown earlier.

Now, you are paying a price for the company based on its operating fundamentals and also based on improvements that you stand to deliver.

EBITDA Valuation Multiples

It is commonplace for articles on M&A to discuss company business valuations as being a multiple of earnings before interest, taxes, depreciation, and amortization (EBITDA). In fact, corporate EBITDA valuation multiples are commonly spoken of as if they represented effective valuation benchmarks. Perhaps this might be the case for companies having similar business model characteristics. However, my view is that EBITDA multiples are simply numbers derived from the three-step business valuation approach illustrated at the beginning of this chapter. One obvious reason for this is that EBITDA multiples are based on accounting conventions, whereas the three-step process shown earlier is a financial construct. Finance always rules.

One shortfall of the use of accounting-driven conventions like EBITDA multiples pertains to the issue of lease capital OPM proceeds. While some companies elect to own their real estate and equipment, others will prefer to lease it from companies similar to the ones I have helped lead. Since the computation for EBITDA is after rent expense, the resultant valuation multiple will exclude the proceeds from lease OPM providers, making the company's EBITDA valuation multiple appear smaller. Conversely, companies owning and financing their real estate and equipment will often appear to

the Countrywide purchase topped $50 billion, wiping out an estimated two thirds of its earnings on every other line of its combined business since the acquisition.[6] Not only did Bank of America endure losses from Countrywide's operations, but it endured a myriad of lawsuits and regulatory actions arising from

Countrywide's activities prior to the bank's ownership.

Time Warner + America Online. In 2000, before the bloom was yet off the dot-com bubble, Time Warner, an established publishing, media, and cable TV powerhouse, elected to take a strategic leap. Their target was America Online, an early internet pioneer that delivered dial-up internet access to over 20 million clients, providing an early taste of the potential for email and internet searches.[7] The method was the largest merger in history. Through the merger, AOL acquired Time Warner for $182 billion in stock and assumed debt, allowing Time Warner shareholders to own 45% of the combined enterprise, though they would be initially contributing 70% of the consolidated company profits. Time Warner's chief executive officer, Gerald Levin, retained his title for the combined company, while Steve Case, AOL's chief executive officer, assumed the role of chairman.

The merger euphoria was short-lived. At the time of the merger, customers with emerging broadband technology amounted to a scant 3% of total internet users, a number that seemed inconsequential to AOL with its monthly subscription business model built on ubiquitous telephone dial-up technology. But fast and powerful broadband quickly supplanted clunky dial-up.[8] That Time Warner's leadership missed this technology trend was ironic, since the company would eventually benefit from the sale of broadband services as one of the nation's major cable TV providers.

Google, which would ultimately offer consumers superior internet search services for free, realized its first profits the year following the merger consummation. Another year later and AOL-Time Warner incurred an eye-popping $99 billion goodwill business valuation write-down. (Remember that accounting non-cash write-downs like this do nothing to alter actual business investment, but rightly signal the lower equity returns realized from poor investment decisions.) With AOL bleeding subscribers and subscription revenues, the company's equity market valuation plummeted over 90% from $226 billion to just $20 billion.

Prior to the merger, the equity valuation of Time Warner stood at north of $80 billion, meaning that the merger ultimately cost its own shareholders nearly 90% of their company value. AOL would eventually be sold to Verizon for the paltry price of $4.4 billion in 2015 before ultimately being jettisoned at a further loss to a private equity firm in 2021.

M&A failures are generally not explosively high profile, as in the case of the Countrywide Mortgage and AOL mergers. In both of those cases, it could be argued that the buyers overlooked various potential catastrophic risk threats. In the case of Bank of America, it was the risk of stepping into the corporate liability shoes of Countrywide Mortgage, a result of Countrywide becoming a wholly owned corporate subsidiary. In the case of Time Warner, it was understanding the massive industry disruption posed by broadband and the viability of a subscription business model in the face of future competitors offering superior services for free.

However, even with these two poster children of bad M&A decisions, one thing should stand out: Despite their gargantuan M&A-driven losses, both companies managed to survive. Both were large, highly capitalized public companies. The same cannot be said for private concerns, which comprise the vast majority of businesses in the United States. With most companies, poor M&A decision-making and integration has a higher potential to be catastrophic.

GE and M&A-Driven Growth

In August of 2001, I was serving as president of Franchise Finance Corporation of America (FFCA), a publicly traded New York Stock Exchange listed REIT. That month, we closed our sale of the company to a subsidiary of GE Capital. The acquisition of FFCA by General Electric (GE) would be the final corporate purchase under the watch of Jack Welch, a leadership icon who had guided the growth of GE since 1981. During his tenure, the company made approximately 1,000 such acquisitions,[9] which were key to GE's

Credit: Forbes magazine

growth strategy and which had helped to drive GE's share price to more than 45 times its 1981 value, or nearly $60 when they first approached us in 2000 to propose the acquisition. M&A activity was so much a part of GE's business model that each company division had its own business development group, which specialized in prospecting, valuing, bidding, acquiring, and integrating target companies.

Key to GE's M&A strategy was to purchase companies having current market equity returns higher than GE's. That way, the acquired businesses would help to elevate GE's market equity return and, along with it, GE's share price, assuming the market equity return demanded by GE shareholders remained the same.

While I prefer to speak of market current equity returns, stock investors might speak instead of share price/earnings multiples, which is the dominant valuation benchmark employed among equity investors. In my view, corporate valuation price/earnings multiples, like EBITDA multiples, are accounting-based derived numbers, with market and current equity returns ultimately lying at the center of business valuation.

M&A-driven earnings per share growth achieved through P/E multiple arbitrage is an old game. Conglomerates, of which GE was a prominent example, have historically been especially adept players because they are generally willing to buy such a wide array of businesses. During the 1960s, a number of conglomerates bearing names like names like LTV, ITT, Litton, Tyco, and Teledyne succeeded in realizing the illusion of earnings growth through a steady stream of corporate acquisitions that benefited from P/E multiple arbitrage. By the late 1960s, public company mergers were averaging 150 a month, with most of the most valuable companies in America characterized as conglomerates.[10] In 1968, the peak year of the "conglomerate boom," public U.S. corporations completed approximately 4,500 mergers, a stunning record.[11]

Around the time that we announced GE's intent to buy FFCA, GE's shares were valued at nearly 40 times trailing earnings. Meanwhile, we were acquired for a substantially lower multiple, meaning that GE's shareholders would benefit from the added value created by multiplying our earnings by the wide differences in our respective multiples. More than that, GE Capital, the finance subsidiary that acquired us, had a far more advantageous capital stack benefiting from less costly borrowings and a far greater use of OPM. Overlaying GE's capital stack onto FFCA served to reduce the acquisition P/E multiple further, contributing to greater earnings per share contribution from the acquisition. Of course, FFCA was small relative to a large company like GE. I estimate that the acquisition contributed well less than 1% to corporate earnings. But, add FFCA to an average of nearly 50 annually acquired companies during Jack Welch's tenure, and M&A stood to materially move the earnings growth needle. Indeed, it could be said that M&A activity proved important to the achievement of steady corporate earnings growth that was noted for its consistency under Welch. How much could the growth be? The simplistic table that follows does a good job illustrating the earnings growth impact of M&A activity. With target company acquisitions representing 10% of corporate enterprise value annually and a 15X multiple difference, earnings per share growth of better than 8% could be produced.

Acquiror Earnings Accretion from Positive P/E Multiple Acquisitions

		Percent of Company Represented by Target				
		10.0%	20.0%	30.0%	40.0%	50.0%
Acquiror Multiple Over Target	1.0X	0.6%	1.3%	2.1%	3.3%	5.0%
	5.0X	2.8%	6.3%	10.7%	16.7%	25.0%
	10.0X	5.6%	12.5%	21.4%	33.3%	50.0%
	15.0X	8.3%	18.8%	32.1%	50.0%	75.0%
	20.0X	11.1%	25.0%	42.9%	66.7%	100.0%

M&A-driven earnings per share growth can generally be expected to last about a year, which generally means that more companies must be acquired in subsequent years to maintain the appearance of continuous growth. Of course, it also helps if the acquired companies are achieving rapid growth in their businesses.

In the case of FFCA, GE received help from M&A accounting that added to the initial multiple arbitrage. In purchasing a company, the assets of the acquired business must be appraised and then recorded on the financial statement of the acquiror for their fair market value. The difference, if any, between the company purchase price and the fair market value of its assets is recorded as "goodwill," which is an intangible asset. In our case, we held thousands of real estate locations that each had to be valued. GE preferred a low (conservative) valuation because cheaper real estate would result in less annual depreciation expense, which would, in turn, elevate future reported earnings. Given cheap real estate, more of the M&A value of FFCA would rest in "goodwill," which was fine because the intangible asset did not have to be amortized, or expensed, which would also stand to improve future reported earnings.

There was one last benefit to marking the real estate with a low value: Eventually, the same real estate could be sold off at elevated gains that would further drive future corporate earnings. GE engaged in material asset sales, which elevated current earnings at the cost of future earnings, since the assets would no longer be there to contribute to future revenues. The gains they reported from this activity were not indicative of their prowess of "buying low and selling high," since they were aided by purchase accounting methodology that shifted much of the purchase value to goodwill. Accounting results can potentially obscure financial results, but only for so long.

GE's Share Performance from 1981 to 2019

Interestingly, six years after we sold FFCA to GE Capital, we would sell our second public company to a private equity consortium that sought a high real estate valuation for its M&A purchase accounting treatment. Their reasoning was to avoid the appearance that they had paid more money for our company than the real estate was worth. The result would be a corporate acquisition that recorded elevated asset values while having negligible goodwill. Over the following years, the high prices recorded for the real estate would result in reduced reported corporate profitability resulting from higher depreciation expenses.

As you saw in the prior chapter, the linkage between the valuation forces of public company equity returns and share performance is not always immediate. Part of the issue is centered in accounting noise which can cloud long-term business model attributes. In the case of highly active acquisitors like GE, the underlying business model and intrinsic growth becomes harder to see. Accounting can make this worse because there is such a wide latitude in how assets are valued, which can result in further near-term distortion. However, business model fundamentals, even of complex conglomerates like GE, ultimately become visible.

Once the acquisition-fueled growth stopped and the tenure of Jack Welch ended, GE's performance began to descend. Between 1981 and the end of 2001, GE's shares had increased in value by over 30X, while the dividend had grown 8.5X to 17 cents per share. I and others at FFCA were handed impressive and frameable stock option certificates giving us the right to buy GE shares at a fixed price of $44 over the ensuing 10 years.

Alas, GE's share price would not see $44 again. In June of 2018, GE became the last of the original members of the Dow Jones Industrial Average to be removed from the venerable stock index it had occupied for more than a century. A year later, GE's shares stood at a valuation of a little over $10, with a dividend at half the 1981 amount at the start of Jack Welch's tenure. Meanwhile, the company's credit rating fell eight notches from AAA to BBB+, while many of the 1,000 companies purchased during Jack Welch's tenure were jettisoned.

GE Capital, which had been a potent engine central to GE's consistent earnings growth, had been reduced to a fraction of its size, with remaining activities centered on providing financing to GE customers for GE-produced products. FFCA, along with the other GE Capital-acquired companies that became parts of GE Franchise Finance, was eventually sold off in pieces.

With all GE's divestitures, revenues in 2020 were roughly 40% lower than they were at the time of our 2001 acquisition and nearly 60% less than their 2008 all-time high. The final chapter of GE's incredible shrinking act was ultimately written by Larry Culp, the first outsider to ever become Chief Executive Officer of the storied company. In November 2021, the downsized company announced that it would split into three separate publicly traded companies, with activities centered in aviation, healthcare, and power delivery. With that defining conclusion, GE's days as a conglomerate were over.

In an irony not lost on any of us at STORE, we moved our offices in 2016 to a building originally constructed by GE to house FFCA's disbanded successor company.

Focusing on What Matters

While Jack Welch averaged 50 corporate acquisitions annually over his tenure at GE, Warren Buffett, the legendary founder and leader of Berkshire Hathaway, in forging his successful conglomerate, averaged fewer than two annually. Unlike GE, Berkshire Hathaway had a holding company model in which the home office had scant staff, with each of the many corporate subsidiaries guided by their own capable leadership. In the course of producing compound annual rates of return of approximately 20% between 1965 and the end of 2020, Warren Buffett gained a deserved reputation as one of the finest stock pickers of all time, with Berkshire having realized outsized returns from a number of prescient public stock investments.

To my way of thinking, this is only partly true. Warren Buffett also proved very talented at corporate acquisitions, with large portions of Berkshire Hathaway's earnings delivered by wholly owned companies like See's Candies, insurer Geico, Berkshire Reinsurance, and Burlington Northern Santa Fe Railroad. With a strong AA-rated balance sheet and ample liquidity, Berkshire was able to advance $3 billion in needed liquidity to cash-strapped GE during the Great Recession in October 2008. The money was in the form of redeemable preferred shares yielding 10% annually, with added warrants to buy GE shares at a fixed price in the future. Between the dividends, the 10% preferred share redemption premium, and more than $300 million in profits from share sales, Berkshire Hathaway realized annual returns in excess of 15% from its GE investment, while GE's common shareholders received paltry returns by comparison.

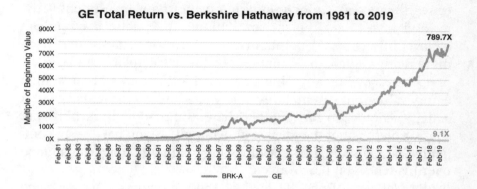

GE Total Return vs. Berkshire Hathaway from 1981 to 2019

Public companies, which include some of the nation's largest concerns, but which comprise about .1% of all US businesses, are not like the rest of corporate America in many ways. Accounting noise and animal spirits abound, and leadership and investors can be tempted to focus on comparatively short-term results. I have remarked often that the attention span of many investors is shorter than a round of golf. Given such short-term views, forces of growth, momentum, and national economic indicators can have a profound impact on share valuations. We have likewise witnessed share valuation moves simply because our company became included in an index of similar sized businesses.

Apart from selling two public companies, our leadership teams have historically avoided M&A activity. The reasons have generally related to suitability and to the impact of such acquisitions on our long-term growth. Over the short run—generally over one to two years—acquisitions can often look enticing. However, over the long term, they can often detract from growth. With that said, real estate investment trusts like STORE make asset investments every day, which can be thought of in the same way as an M&A transaction. Every real estate asset purchased has an investment amount, an operating profit margin, and is funded by a mix of OPM and equity. As a result, our companies prepared pricing models to understand what the expected rates of return are for the investments we made. While the companies I have helped lead have had a proud history of working to take a long-term approach to our investment activity and investment return expectations, the public markets can behave differently. At points in time where our shares have been more richly valued, the signal sent by the marketplace can be interpreted to say, "Buy anything and buy a lot!" That is because high equity valuations can make even low yielding investments or M&A activity accretive to earnings per share. But producing earnings per share growth is not the ideal goal. After all, as you have seen, companies can actually grow earnings per share while lighting a good chunk of value on fire.

The primary financial goal of the companies I have helped guide has always been to create value as measured by compound EMVA growth. Our view here has been that, like the rest of corporate America and over the long term, there is a valuation vortex around equity returns. Water always seeks its own level. Only with public companies, this can often take some time.

Chapter 14
The Essential Ingredient

Without question, equity returns lie at the heart of corporate wealth creation. In turn, quality business models lie at the heart of corporate equity returns. Such business models are conceived, adopted, and executed by founding corporate entrepreneurs and business leaders, often with material assists from company management and staff. While much of the focus on this book is centered on the financial dynamics and basics of corporate wealth creation, business models do not execute themselves. Human effort drives business model creation and execution. It is the essential ingredient.

The Growing Restaurant Illustration

In chapter 10, to illustrate the power of OPM equity, I presented a case of a growing restaurant enterprise. The sample company starts with a single location funded with YOM and OPM in year one, adding a second location in year two funded with OPM equity and OPM. Over the next three years, the company adds another eight locations that are funded with retained equity cash flows and OPM. The case study is feasible, and I have witnessed companies successfully embark on similar aggressive growth strategies.

Do not take my rosy corporate scenario to mean that I believe execution to be easy. There are more restaurant locations in the world than any other service or retail establishment. The restaurant industry is mature and highly competitive, with new restaurant successes typically won at the cost of market share taken from other restaurant locations. In a broader sense, restaurants also compete for a "share of stomach" with supermarkets, convenience stores, movie theaters, and other participants. Gaining and keeping restaurant market share is hard.

Whereas entrepreneurs engaged in mature industries like the restaurant industry tend to be driven by grabbing a piece of the market share pie, novel business enterprises aim to get in on the ground floor of pie creation. Both strategies have distinctive execution risks, and both are capable of EMVA creation.

While there are just six financial variables that collectively comprise corporate business models, there are nearly infinite operational alternatives that stand behind the numbers and the resultant equity returns. This universal truth demands capable leadership. When it comes to the restaurant industry, the following provides a small flavor of the many operational considerations that need to be addressed in conceiving a viable business model:

1. Hours of operation: What are your hours of operation? Do you serve breakfast, lunch, and dinner? Are you open seven days a week?
2. Menu offerings: How many menu offerings do you have?
3. Beverages: Do you serve alcoholic beverages?
4. Service: Do you have no-, partial-, or full-table service?
5. Take out: Do you have a drive-thru window or other means to pick up food to go?
6. Delivery: Do you deliver food or partner with food delivery services?
7. Internet: Do you have online ordering or reservations?
8. Reservations: Do you accept table reservations?
9. Staffing and management: How much staffing and management do you require?
10. Advertising: How much and what type of advertising might you need?

Restaurants, like nearly all businesses, are complex, involving hundreds of operational design considerations. Restaurants are also people intensive, with labor typically representing the greatest financial burden. It follows that labor effectiveness is absolutely impacted by the quality of training, the level of staff motivation, the corporate goals established and the financial incentives to achieve those goals, all of which are reflections of corporate leadership and its strategic vision.

Business operational strategies are never as simple as the Six Variable financial business model they ultimately form. Monty Williams joined my hometown NBA team, the Phoenix Suns, in 2019 as their head coach and is fond of saying, "Everything you want is on the other side of hard."

EMVA creation can be like that.

Designed Structural Change

I have been fortunate to have the opportunity to contribute to the creation of three corporate business models. Each of the three companies we created was engaged in a similar business: all owned real estate across the country integral to the operations of our many tenants. Because we conceived each company, we were able to design their operating models at the outset. And because each company was in a similar line of business, we were able to learn from our prior experiences to improve our business models with each successive corporate formation.

Our earliest company grew to manage approximately $6 billion in real estate assets prior to its eventual 2001 sale to GE Capital. We were vertically integrated at the time, having more than 200 employees directly engaged in an array of activities, from new business origination to portfolio management. We had staff that monitored the insurance and property taxes at each location. We had a complete information technology team, including full-time programmers, to create and manage our proprietary portfolio servicing and accounting platforms. We had what amounted to an internal law firm, with lawyers and paralegals helping us with legal matters arising from our complex business activities. At the heart of our organization was an impressive sales team capable of originating and closing well over $1 billion in new investments annually. At the time we sold our organization to GE Capital, we believed our operating model was the state of the art.

Scarcely two years later, when we had the chance to start our second company, we changed our minds and radically altered our organizational structure. Technology had changed and so had our personal perspective. So, we set about to implement a series of designed structural modifications:

Technology-Enabled Changes

We are fortunate to live in an era characterized by rapid technological advances that can have profound impacts on corporate operational models. With change a given, all businesses should be in a constant state of technological reevaluation as they seek out potential efficiencies.

I learned this early on in my career, when I persuaded the president of the bank that employed me to buy its first ever personal computer. That device was used to spread the corporate financial statements of bank customers and launched me on my path to better understand corporate business models. Since then, the pace of technological change has been blinding, which has had a profound impact on corporate business models.

One of the first things we decided to do when starting our second company was to outsource nearly all our information technology needs. We still had a server on site, but it was relegated to a closet together with our telephone infrastructure. Gone were the days where I could show off a massive computer and backup tape array sitting on an elevated cooled floor and protected by a halon fire extinguisher. Information technology had changed, with increasing platform standardization and integration that made it feasible to outsource. In doing so, we eliminated a high fixed cost, converting it to a reduced variable cost.

We also decided to outsource the administrative aspects of portfolio servicing, including rent collections, together with the monitoring of property taxes and insurance. Our earliest monitoring platform was largely designed in the 1980s. However, the commercial mortgage-backed securities (CMBS) market emerged in 1990, toward the conclusion of the Savings and Loan Crisis and inspired by the success of residential mortgage securitizations. Basically, this meant that loans against commercial real estate were pooled, tranched, rated, and sold off to institutional fixed income investors. But for this to happen required the emergence of professional portfolio servicing companies, who would remit the payments to the investors and monitor the loan portfolios. What were three of the major functions performed by these servicing companies? You got it; they collected payments and monitored real estate taxes and property insurance policies. We approached a few of these companies to see if they might be willing to provide a similar service for a portfolio of leased real estate. In taking this approach, we again took large, fixed costs, converting them to smaller variable costs. Outsourcing these labor and systems intensive tasks also had the benefit of improved security and controls that we and our OPM providers welcomed.

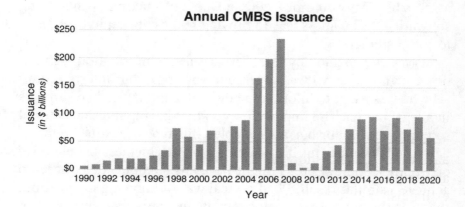

SOURCES: Data from Chandan Economics and J.P. Morgan Securities and Commercial Real Estate Direct

Core Competency Refinement

Core competencies are defined as identified essential skills tethered to the problems and stakeholders that businesses are designed to address.

Companies tend to be best off if they can identify and refine their core competencies and focus on them with minimal distraction. Simply deciding on core competency focus requires discipline and can take some time. Fortunately, we had time, starting our version 2.0 investment platform more than 20 years after the first.

Information technology and legal services were not our core competency. I was a businessperson and a finance professional and so reasonably uninformed when it came to the evaluation of the effectiveness of our IT and legal services departments.

One day, the head of our network administration came into my office and made a pitch: He wanted a SANS system (SANS stands for SysAdmin, Audit, Network, and Security) to improve the redundancy and security of our company's IT infrastructure. The cost was $1 million, and his proposal was supported by the department head. I was lost. However, I approved the investment, making a vow to one day figure out how to outsource as much of the IT function as possible. We were not in the business of making or marketing software. Our business was to provide real estate capital solutions to our customers.

I was as mystified by legal services as by information technology. On another day I was approached by one of our internal counsel who was eager to inform me how much money he had saved us in a legal matter. The implication was that having internal counsel so familiar with our business enabled this type of result. I remember simply wondering if I were one of the luckiest people alive or whether, somewhere, I might have engaged outside counsel to achieve a similar result. I had no real way of knowing for sure, but that was the point. In a small company like ours, I felt unqualified to lead or assess an internal law firm. Like IT, this could never be a core competency.

When we started our second company, we had a single general counsel and no legal department.

One of the risks in our business is that we make investments with documentation and terms not matching our initial transaction approval. All finance companies bear this risk. In banking, they have personnel devoted to the review of extended loans to be certain that they were funded as initially approved. We had a similar department in our earliest company. The problem for us was that, unlike a bank, we had far less ability to influence our customers to make subsequent changes in the event of an error. So, we arrived at a solution to eliminate the quality control department. Instead, we elected to have our outsourced external legal counsel certify that the transactions they closed conformed with the terms of our approval. Quality would be built into our investment process up front where it mattered most.

Our earliest company also had an investor relations department, which stemmed from our history of having raised our earliest capital directly from retail investors through the stockbrokers they used. However, given greater corporate communication regulatory complexity, together with our changing investor landscape, we elected to also outsource this function. Unlike our other outsourcing endeavors, doing so did not save money or materially add to our operating efficiency. It simply made us better and again acknowledged a function that could not be a core competency.

We made one more key organizational change. We redesigned our sales force to have no direct reports. Salespeople are always among the most valued professionals in any organization. At our earliest platform, our investment origination professionals each oversaw support personnel, who they hired as needed. Given that expanded teams of people was costless to our commissioned salesforce, representing a miserable alignment of interest, we had two choices: We could make each sales territory a profit center, charging them for their resources, or we could simplify their organization structure, shifting their support staff to other departments. We selected the simpler second option.

We also made a material OPM change, choosing to abandon the corporate investment-grade rating and unsecured borrowing approach pioneered by our earliest platform in favor of a flexible investment-grade secured financing approach that we developed. That served to slightly elevate our OPM mix, increasing our ROE and making our capital stack fully assumable, which proved important in delivering shareholder returns upon the eventual 2007 company sale.

Four years later, we started STORE Capital, which would be version 3.0 of our real estate net lease strategy. Our chosen name, which stands for Single Tenant Operational Real Estate, represented an investment focus refinement; we elected to invest in only commercial freestanding profit center properties. We also elected to have a far more diverse investment portfolio. When it came to our operations, we retained all our prior version 2.0 modifications, adding a few more designed structural modifications, including:

- Outsourcing tenant financial statement capture, turning a fixed cost into a variable cost.
- Improving the integration of our IT systems with our outsourced service providers.
- Segmenting our origination team between direct and broker-originated opportunities.
- Adding a portfolio management department.
- Moving to exclusively cloud-based computing solutions,
- Increasing resources dedicated to investment origination activities.
- Using complementary secured and unsecured investment-grade OPM.

Technology-enabled enhancements continued to play a role in our operating model evolution. Now we no longer even had a computer server in the closet. Together with the systems and software we employed, our computer platforms were housed in multiple off-site data centers. This evolution will have a lasting impact on STORE's ability to execute future operational enhancements.

One of the key takeaways gained from starting our second platform was the importance of designing and establishing a strong and flexible IT foundation from the start. With version 2.0, our founding private OPM equity investors expected us to file for an initial public offering a mere six months after having raised our first equity capital. We did so, publicly listing the company almost exactly a year from the date we officially opened our doors for business. This rapid scheduling contributed to an oversight. We started our company on an insufficiently robust IT platform, spending insufficient time on overall system design. Over time, this shortcoming would result in elevated costs, from personnel to time to the ultimate need to implement and design a complete system conversion.

Lesson learned.

Collectively, the version 2.0 and 3.0 designed operational enhancements we made were impactful. By the end of 2020, STORE Capital managed nearly twice the amount of capital of our earliest operating platform, but with about half the staff. But numbers do not tell the whole story. Our staff mix included more sales, credit, and closing professionals than our earliest platform, serving to give us far more potent business origination capabilities. What is more, having outsourced most administrative tasks, our staff was now largely comprised of professionals.

Keeping It Simple

Operational changes, like the ones we have executed over the years, are broadly designed to lower business investment needs, elevate operating profit margins and improve capital efficiency. They are also designed to improve the simplicity of the corporate operating model, while allowing the business to focus on what we are good at: Our core competencies.

One of my business model observations is that companies are like organic life forms. The founders hire the earliest staff. In turn, assuming the company is successful and starts to grow, those employees hire other employees. Eventually, your expanded staff begins to make organizational adjustments. Ten years after co-founding STORE, there were many aspects of our processes in which I had little personal input. However, the essential organizational structure conceived by me, and the other STORE founders remained in place. So did the basic potent business model we created. They are effectively the canvas on which future leaders paint.

Peter Drucker
Credit: George Rose/Hulton Archive/
Getty Images

In his groundbreaking 1946 book *The Concept of the Corporation*, management pioneer Peter Drucker keenly observed, "No institution can possibly survive if it needs geniuses or supermen to manage it. It must be organized in such a way as to be able to get along under a leadership composed of average human beings."

I agree. With fewer employees and fewer departments, our goal over the years has been to simplify a business organization structure to be more centered on our core competencies and corporate objectives.

A clear benefit of well-crafted business organization structures is that they tend to broadly distribute leadership responsibilities, giving senior executives more time to attend to strategic planning and initiatives. When it comes to the daily corporate administration within a potent business organization, senior executives become less important. I have seen this first-hand. Members of the leadership team that started STORE Capital collectively departed our predecessor company without being replaced for nearly two years. The version 2.0 business we founded and the operational model we launched functioned well, eventually enabling the company to be reintroduced to the public markets.

In 1954, Peter Ducker famously introduced the concept of "management by objectives" (MBO), the central idea being that key objective determination enables performance measurement and better goal setting. Of course, objectives tend to center around corporate core competencies, and both can take considerable time and thought to develop. In our case, we had that time. At the inception of the operational design changes implemented in our second company, we had a leadership team comprised of members who each had experience with our earliest platform ranging from 10 to more than 20 years. Eight years later, that same team would collectively work on the formation of STORE to create a more refined organizational and operational canvas.

Planned vs. Imposed Structural Change

Business models are forever subject to change. That change can result from planned designed structural change as laid out in the evolution of STORE's corporate model over the years or change can be imposed by external forces. Failing to respond to imposed external changes can risk corporate relevance and survival.

No businesses are immune from externally imposed business model changes. Restaurants are no exception. Dining establishments that have not addressed changing consumer access preferences have paid a price. Smart phone applications, gift cards, and online ordering and reservations are conveniences that consumers have grown to expect. To address rising labor costs, restaurants have implemented solutions ranging from connected computer tablets to varying methods of limited table service to automated labor scheduling, among other innovations. The successful adoption of elevated cost controls or changing consumer access preferences has had a definite impact on the big three business model variables that individually and collectively most impact EMVA creation.

Externally imposed business model changes can be anticipated or unanticipated. The former is definitely best. Unanticipated imposed business model changes can demand a shorter required response time, which can seem to observers to be both reactive and defensive, raising business vulnerability. Business model changes often entail organizational and operational changes, not to mention corporate competency reevaluation, and are best done with the benefit of time.

I have had experience with both unanticipated and anticipated imposed external business model changes. In 1988, we lost our principal source of investment funding with the demise of EF Hutton, a prominent New York City–based investment bank founded in 1904. The company was taken down in short order by a series of criminal indictments. That imposed and unanticipated change would cause us to redirect our fundraising efforts and organization to other investors, a process that both set back our growth and took some time.

Four years later, we set about to address an anticipated imposed change. We embarked on a plan to publicly list the majority of our managed real estate investments. While our investors were not demanding liquidity, we anticipated they would one day hold a different view. So, we embarked on a move to take our first company public. The entire process entailed some risk, took two years to accomplish, and holds the record of the largest real estate partnership roll-up ever completed. Our successful public listing would naturally have profound changes on our operational and business model.

A key part of business leadership is staying on top of externally imposed changes, trying to avoid unanticipated surprises. I'd like to think our leadership teams have done a pretty good job of this over the years, but I am fond of telling a story about dodging one such bullet.

In 1996, two years after taking our first company public, I was sitting in a law office at Two World Trade Center. I was there to close our inaugural secured bond issuance, the proceeds of which were used to finance a pool of chain store mortgages we had extended to our customers. The amount of the bond issuance was approximately $180 million, a material amount, and I prepared to sign a sea of papers that were organized on a board table, standing tall in a cascade of aluminum accordion document holders. But as

I entered the room, it became clear that the assembled investment bankers, lawyers, and accountants were nervous and I was about to learn why.

Our bond tax counsel entered the room to inform me that there was a risk that we would be unable to close the transaction. In fact, there was a risk that we would have to return the bond proceeds to the investors that we had successfully solicited. Such an outcome would have been both painful and embarrassing, and so I began to run through alternatives in my mind. I also began to wonder how I could possibly be caught facing unanticipated externally imposed change given the many experts we had engaged. The reason for this predicament was pending tax legislation that was to potentially be included in a tax bill set to emerge from the House Ways and Means Committee that afternoon. So, we were told that we should just be prepared to wait until the bill emerged. At the time, I was comforted to know that our investment banking, legal, and accounting experts were willing to use their extensive government relations staffs to uncover the answer as soon as possible. With nothing else to do, we went to lunch.

Upon our return, no progress had been made and the chairman of the House Ways and Means Committee had yet to emerge with proposed tax legislation. At the time, cell phones and email were emerging and not yet a business fixture. Google would be founded a few months later. But this was a fancy law firm and there was a phone booth. So, I went in, dialed the number for directory assistance and requested the phone number for the House of Representatives. With that number, I telephoned Congress and asked if I might be put through to the House Ways and Means Committee room. The receptionist put me through, and a legislative aid picked up the phone. I then presented my predicament and asked if he had knowledge about the specific tax issues that had the potential to kill our pending bond issuance. He did and told me that I needn't worry and that we should be good to proceed with our bond closing. Of course, I required some evidence and so he kindly faxed me the appropriate language from the pending tax legislation.

We quickly closed the bond issuance, and I was grateful to have avoided an unanticipated externally imposed change. And I naturally felt self-satisfied, having found an answer that had eluded the many knowledgeable experts we had engaged. I also felt encouraged that I could cold call Congress and find people there kind enough to stop what they were doing for a moment to help me. We had failed to see the potential for externally imposed change coming. But, faced with this reality, I did what is expected of leaders: I took the initiative to find a solution.

One of the most common questions public company business executives get is this: "What keeps you awake at night?" We have done our level best to sleep well across the three public companies we have guided. That said, unanticipated externally imposed changes loom large when it comes to business risk. Over the years, such events can be impactful, from our early E.F. Hutton experience, to the savings and loan crisis around the same time to the 1998 demise of Long Term Capital Management, the dot-com implosion two years later, the great recession eight years after that and the global pandemic that began in 2020. Unanticipated externally imposed change is a constant force that demands business model prudence and material margins for error.

Blockbuster Video

When it comes to a failure to respond to anticipated externally imposed change, former video rental pioneer Blockbuster Video stands tall. The first Blockbuster location opened in Dallas, Texas, in 1985, with the company becoming publicly listed a year later. In 1987, the company was taken over and led by serial entrepreneur Wayne Huizenga o, through franchising, corporate store development and acquisi-, grew the chain to more than 3,700 video rental and another sic store locations by the end of 1994. With company revenues hing $3 billion, Huizenga anticipated imposed change was rizon. He had concerns about video on demand and the tency of cable television. At the end of 1994, Huizenga guided Blockbuster to a merger with diversified media giant Viacom for an equity value of $8.4 billion that proved valuable. When he died in 2018, he ranked inside the top 300 richest people in America, with a reported net worth approaching $3 billion.

Huizenga's successor at Blockbuster was former Taco Bell CEO John Antioco, who continued the company's rapid rise, growing the number of locations to more than 9,000 by 2004. However, he also saw that change was coming. The advent of DVD technology resulted in higher levels of movie sales. It also made it feasible to rent movies by sending DVDs through the mail. That was the idea of Netflix founder Reed Hastings, who approached Antioco in 2000 to sell his nascent and money losing company for $50 million.[1] Blockbuster had an asset-heavy business model with many retail locations throughout the world. By contrast, Netflix employed a more asset-light model. Given Blockbuster's customer base, the Netflix model could be expected to become profitable more rapidly. But it would come at an enormous cost to Blockbuster's existing business model and franchisee base, entailing substantial and painful changes. Blockbuster declined, and Netflix went public in 2002. Two years later, Viacom, electing to not address Blockbuster's challenges, spun off the vulnerable business unit into a freestanding public company.

The future of video watching did not reside in Blockbuster's rental model. But it was not in the rental by mail Netflix business model, either. It centered in video on demand, which Netflix began to roll out in 2007. Likewise, Blockbuster introduced its Total Access online rental service the same year in a $1 billion promotional campaign. The costs to make such a business model change were enormous and were accentuated by the company's decision to abandon its unpopular late fees. At its height, video rental late fees amounted to more than 15% of Blockbuster's revenues, but an even greater portion of earnings, since they fell straight to the bottom. Activist shareholder Carl Icahn was displeased, gained three board seats in a proxy battle, and ultimately installed a new CEO who abandoned the transition to online rentals. With the playing for online video rentals ceded to Netflix, Blockbuster filed for bankruptcy protection a mere three years later.

Sometimes companies have a hard time responding to antici-pated, externally imposed change. The costs to respond can be enormous and the changes to the operational and business mod-els gut-wrenching. Eastman Kodak ironically created the instru-ment of its own externally imposed change when it patented the first digital camera in 1975. During the twentieth century, Kodak dominated the global sales of camera film and film processing. Competing with its own lucrative film leadership to promote and invest in a technology having an uncertain business model proved elusive. The company filed for bankruptcy protection in 2012, scarcely more than two years following the demise of Blockbuster.

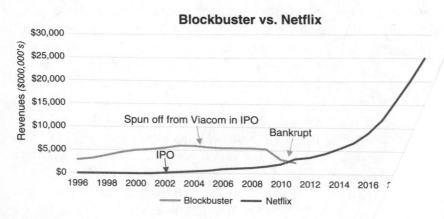

Blockbuster vs. Netflix

SOURCE: Data from Corporate SEC Filings

Anticipated, externally imposed changes are ' verbial train light coming at you in a long, dark t see the train coming, but often have no idea ho As real estate investors in our earliest compan eventual closure of Blockbuster stores, if not t of the company. But the changes happened f tially expected.

Technological change lies at the center ness model changes. As I write this, the ket share taken by electric vehicles, as driverless vehicles, are just two technologies that will have repercussions across many industries. Sometimes imposed business model changes result from governmental actions, which can include environmental regulatory changes, or alterations in tax and tariff frameworks, just to name a few. When external imposed changes happen, they compel any number of industries to adapt or risk their relevance. As Blockbuster and Kodak demonstrate, the anticipated imposed changes required can occasionally be simply too painful to execute.

Designed Revolutionary Change

It is highly risky for businesses to radically alter their business models mid-stream. But every now and then, businesses embark on successful designed changes to their business models that are revolutionary.

In 1997, with the company suffering losses, Apple invited its co-founder and original visionary Steve Jobs to return. A year later, the company introduced its inaugural iMac computer, resulting in the company posting its first profit since 1995. The all-in-one design and ease of use of this compelling computer, which came in an array of colors, helped sustain Apple's near-term profitability. Earnings were also bolstered by the company's difficult decision to discontinue its unprofitable Newton product, an early personal digital assistant that incorporated handwriting recognition. In 1999, earnings nearly doubled before retrenching to a small loss in 2001. But despite the loss, 2001 would arguably prove to be Apple's most significant and momentous year, setting the groundwork for radical improvements in its future business model.

Over an eight-month period in 2001, Apple designed and introduced the iPod, an MP3 player that would revolutionize the digitized music industry. In January of the same year, the company announced the creation of iTunes, with the first Apple Store introduced four months later.[2] Collectively, these moves set the foundation for Apple's eventual leadership in establishing an integrated entertainment environment. Five years later, the company's iPod sales approached $8 billion, amounting to almost 40% of corporate revenues. And 10 years after it was introduced, cumulative iPod unit sales exceeded 300 million, representing an eye-popping 78% market share of portable digital media sales.[3]

In 2007, another momentous year, Apple introduced its groundbreaking iPhone product, which would ultimately "featurize" iPod capabilities, incorporating them inside an appealing, cutting edge and feature-laden smartphone. As a result, iPod sales predicably declined, falling to 1% of company revenues over the next seven years, while iPhone revenues rose to more than 55% of company revenues. Three years after launching the iPhone, Apple introduced the iPad, a mobile tablet computer resembling in appearance a larger version of the company's successful iPhone. Like the iPhone, the iPad also incorporated the capabilities initially introduced with the iPod, while integrating seamlessly into the company's growing entertainment environment. Meanwhile, iTunes store sales, which were made possible with the 2001 introduction of the iPod, grew to exceed $18 billion, amounting to close to 10% of total revenues. By 2020, iPhone revenues continued to exceed 50% of company revenues, with recurring service revenues, which includes iTunes, growing to over $53 billion, representing nearly 20% of company sales. What was formerly a barely profitable personal computer company upon the return of Steve Jobs in 1997 had been radically transformed, pivoting to a far more potent business model that vaulted Apple into one of the world's most valuable companies.

Apple could no longer be viewed as a personal computer company. By 2020, sales of Mac computers were scarcely more than 10% of corporate revenues.

When asked about Apple's vision, CEO Steve Cook stated in 2009, "We believe that we are on the face of the earth to make great products and that's not changing. We are constantly focusing on innovating."

With these words, Steve Cook put an exclamation point on Apple's continued openness to future designed revolutionary change.

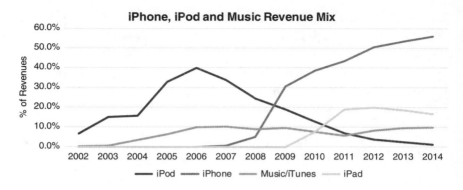

iPhone, iPod and Music Revenue Mix

SOURCE: Data from Company SEC 10-K Filings

Reengineering the Corporation

Embarking on corporate planned or externally imposed changes involves reengineering a company's operational models, ultimately impacting the corporate business model as reflected at a high level by its six financial variables. There's even a name for this: business process reengineering (BPR), a concept credited to Michael Hammer and Thomas Davenport while collaborating professors at

Description: Drs. Michael Hammer and Thomas Davenport, corporate reengineering pioneers.

MIT and Babson respectively in the late 1980s.[4] In 1993, Hammer and co-author James Champy published *Reengineering the Corporation: A Manifesto for Business Revolution*, among the best-selling business books of all time. While the book was highly influential, Hammer and Champy noted that corporate reengineering is difficult, with a modest rate of success not far off from that of public company mergers. The reasons for reengineering failure can be many, ranging from a lack of planning and communication to fears of change and resultant corporate culture impact.

My observation has likewise been that designed structural changes can be transformative, but difficult. Sometimes designed changes occur in response to changes in technology. Sometimes, they occur as business missions and core competencies are refined. Sometimes they occur in response to anticipated imposed external events. Sometimes, a need to reengineer a business model occurs in response to unanticipated imposed external events. Finally, there is always the unfortunate potential for an unanticipated internal event, which typically arises from human error.

I believe that corporate reengineering is best and least risky if it is constantly done. In that light, business model changes tend to be more evolutionary and less revolutionary, with corporate cultures open to constant self-assessment and change. Those cultures might rely on applied business tools, such as Peter Drucker's management by objectives, or Six Sigma, a set of techniques developed at Motorola designed to elevate quality through process changes.

Any process-designed reengineering roadmap is no substitute for thoughtfulness and insight. As Peter Drucker observed, leaders often fail to focus on meaningful objectives in their attempt to implement MBO, making the exercise ineffective. Likewise, Six Sigma process success is centered on defining the right problems to be solved and then having the right people in the room to solve them. I have witnessed failure on both accounts, where the problems to be solved were insufficiently meaningful and where the correct process stakeholders were not included in the exercise.

Reengineering efforts, to be impactful, require an elevated vision and participation from key staff members from across the business, with an aim to address the biggest, most strategic and impactful corporate challenges and opportunities.

No business is immune from a need to constantly reengineer. Certainly, any company undergoing meaningful growth will require a steady diet of process and business model reengineering. Such will be true of the start-up restaurant company in chapter 10 having aggressive plans to grow to 10 units over a brief five-year period. During that period, there will likely be anticipated designed operational changes, together with imposed changes that may be anticipated or unanticipated.

Peter Drucker once stated, "Whenever you see a successful business, someone once made a courageous decision."

I believe that strong successful business cultures are those that never cease to make courageous decisions.

Chapter 15
The Art of the Possible

B y now, you should have a clear idea of the important business model attributes that collectively characterize the finest companies.

At the top of the list is an ability to produce high equity returns. Companies capable of producing the highest returns on equity with the lowest use of OPM tend to be some of the finest vehicles for wealth creation.

If your business is highly scalable and has the potential to harness operating leverage, so much the better.

Finally, if your business has the potential to assume a leadership position within a large global marketplace, then it has the potential to be a veritable unicorn. And, if you are fortunate to be a founder or leader of such a business and have the ability to retain a large ownership stake, then you have the chance to become an individual unicorn.

The vast majority of successful companies do not come close to the business model ideals that might gain you a unicorn ticket to the Forbes 400. For one, most companies do not service the needs of large global markets, instead focusing on narrower constituencies.

Unless your business model is centered on technology or an "asset light" operational approach, you will likely benefit little from operating leverage. In other words, your business model will require business investment growth on a pace closer to your revenue growth if you want to expand. Many companies simply have difficulty scaling to a larger size. Most companies require generous amounts of OPM and OPM equity to realize appealing equity returns. The need for OPM equity can also make it rare for company founders to create big businesses in which they can retain large amounts of personal ownership.

Over 40 years of providing capital to thousands of businesses has given me some perspective on defining wins in business. People make business wins happen, which means that winning in business starts with personal goals and aspirations. In an email blog that I received from Scott Galloway, an entrepreneur, author, and professor of marketing at New York University's Stern School of Business, he made a keen observation:

"People often come to NYU and say, 'Follow your passion' – which is total bulls – especially because the individual telling you to follow your passion usually became magnificently wealthy selling software as a service for the scheduling of health care maintenance workers. And I refuse to believe that that was his or her passion."

Instead, Scott borrows advice from fellow author Malcolm Gladwell, which is to invest 10,000 hours of time to become great what you are good at. Finding out what you are good at can take time, and even benefit from some luck. But I have generally found that people who end up being great at what they do, tend to love what they do and who they eventually become.

In their 2020 survey of high-income millennials, Spectrem Group, a consulting firm that provides counsel to investment advisors, supported Scott Galloway's observation. Most of the top measures of life success listed by the respondents pertained to financial success. Being passionate about the work that gets them there was way down the list.

How Do You Define Success?

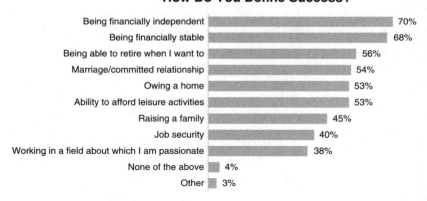

SOURCE: Data from Spectrem Group

The companies I have worked for have helped scores of businesses create value for their equity investors and opportunities for their employees and the communities they serve. We have contributed to many financial success stories. We have helped create financial wins. Yet there has not been a single billionaire created. In fact, we declined the one shot we ever had at providing capital to a company whose founder was to eventually be included in the Forbes 400. Our customers, just like the companies I have helped lead, have had business models that imposed limitations on their personal wealth creation potential. It did not matter. Our businesses and those of most of our customers have created impressive amounts of wealth in the course of doing what we have individually and collectively been good at.

There is not only one winning business model for each of us. We have the potential to take what we are good at and apply this ability to create different and formidable business models.

Just understanding this can improve your personal career options. Companies having strong business models tend to have more highly paid employees, together with better career path options and personal growth prospects. Working for companies having solid business models can also provide a resume boost. Given your personal skills and a choice of places to apply them, why not apply them to a company having a superior business model that can use what you're good at?

The Circles of Business Life

Business models are not static; they change over time. In 1901, Andrew Carnegie sold his steel company for more than $300 million, surpassing John D. Rockefeller for a time to become the richest American. In 2021, there were just 15 members of the Forbes 400 whose business interests were centered in manufacturing, with none of them having interests in steel production.

For his part, John D. Rockefeller, who made his personal fortune in the oil industry, is generally singled out as the richest American in history. Yet just 14 of the 2021 Forbes 400 had net worths centered in oil and gas production and delivery, with all but three ranked over 150 and the richest ranked at number 63.

Financier J.P. Morgan was a dominant force during the Gilded Age, ushering in a wave of corporate consolidations, including the acquisition of Carnegie Steel, which became the foundation for the United States Steel Corporation. By the time he died in 1913, J.P. Morgan was also among the richest Americans, with an estimated net worth approaching $120 million. In an era of rapid economic expansion associated with the second industrial revolution, Morgan was in the company of numerous well-known and wealthy financiers, including Andrew and Richard Mellon, Moses Taylor, James Stillman, George Baker, and more.

You know where this is going: By 2021, the Forbes 400 list of richest Americans included but a single name whose net worth stemmed from banking investments.

While traditional banking has fallen from favor as a source of wealth for the richest among us, nearly a quarter of the 2021 Forbes 400 was otherwise engaged in investments and money management. High-tech entrepreneurs may stand out at the top of the

Forbes 400 listing, but, numerically, investment management enterprises dominate.

It's not that industries like steel, oil, and banking went away. It's that these industries matured. Over generations, growth in these sectors simply slowed and the equity in the associated great companies long ago created by some of our nation's leading business titans became widely held.

Given all the attention drawn to business unicorns associated with new and disruptive technologies, you might be surprised to know that it is commonplace to see highly successful established businesses that would not be built from scratch today. One of the real estate investment metrics STORE Capital regularly examines and discloses is the amount the company pays for real estate investments relative to what they would cost to replace if built today. Quite often, STORE purchases assets for values below their effective replacement costs.

The reasons for this are generally two-fold.

First, the operating profitability of the company using the real estate is simply insufficient to justify the business investment of building such an asset from scratch. Such events can happen for many reasons. The rising cost to construct a new building can outpace the operating cash flow thrown off by the business model. Or the business model may have simply become less potent over time as the company and sector matured.

The second reason is indirectly related to the first: The market rents for similar properties are too low to warrant their construction today.

None of this is a limitation to EMVA creation, though it can impose limits on corporate growth. If you cannot afford to make new business investments at cost, then expansion is most likely to be derived from the acquisition of other, similar existing businesses. Such growth strategies are commonplace within mature industries.

I have always thought of STORE Capital and its predecessor companies as non-bank financial services providers. At the end of 2020, were you to look at the left (asset) side of STORE's balance sheet, you would have seen approximately $10 billion in real estate assets. That might have led you to believe STORE to be a real estate investment company. But the *reason* STORE owned this real estate is more defining. We formed the company to provide lease capital to middle market and larger companies across America for their profit center real estate locations. STORE is an important piece of the OPM capital stack puzzle that its customers assemble as they capitalize their companies. Basically, STORE's customers choose them over banking and other options to finance their real estate.

As an effective finance company, STORE's business model must be sufficiently robust to occasionally absorb losses from tenants suffering business model reverses. All OPM providers strive to have business models having margins of error that enable them to absorb occasional losses and still create meaningful EMVA. During my tenure at STORE, the average recovery we realized on non-performing investments approximated 70%. Losses to us, while unfortunate, generally allowed another business to occupy the real estate at a lower cost. For them, the benefits of a reduced business investment contributed to their own elevated EMVA creation possibilities.

Business models change, new business sectors emerge, and established business sectors commonly see their ownership dispersed over time.

There is also a circle of business life.

In 1893, watch retailer Sears, Roebuck and Co. was an early market disruptor that began selling their products through mail-order catalogues. One year later, the catalogue was more than 300 pages, selling everything from watches to sewing machines, toys, automobiles, and even prefabricated houses, all delivered by rail.[1] In 1906, Sears became a publicly traded company, marking the first initial public offering for a major retail store chain. The company traded under the ticker symbol "S" and was a component of the Dow Jones Industrial Average from 1924 until 1999. When I was growing up, Sears was the country's largest retailer and my parents regularly ordered from their catalogue, which was far bigger than most large urban area phonebooks.

But then came discounters like Walmart and "category kill-ers" like Home Depot and Best Buy, which eroded Sears's competi-tive edge and permanently wounded its once dominant business model. In 1993, the company discontinued the iconic catalogue that had initially vaulted Sears into prominence a hundred years prior. Ironically, a year later, Jeff Bezos would start Amazon, taking a page from Sears's disruptive pioneering innovation. The company began by offering a catalogue for books, only this time the catalogue was paperless and online. Amazon then followed a strategy that paral-leled the successful road map laid out by Richard Sears a century earlier: The company greatly and successfully expanded its retail product offerings, which would prove damaging to the business models of Sears and many other retailers.

After years of declining sales and encroaching competition, Sears filed for Chapter 11 bankruptcy protection on October 15, 2018.

Business models come and go, and the dynamics of their changes are reflected in our overall economic dynamism.

As Benjamin Franklin said, "When you're finished changing, you're finished."

Oftentimes, companies suffering business model reverses can be revived. Oaktree Capital, a principal founding institutional investor in STORE Capital, got its start as a distressed debt invest-ment management firm. Basically, its initial strategy was to buy in the debt of distressed companies, which was sold to them at dis-counted prices by their initial lenders. Key to this strategy was a general belief in the business model potential of the companies whose debt Oaktree would own. Should the company reverse its performance slide, then the debt would be repaid, allowing Oaktree to earn interest income and make a profit by realizing the gain between the discounted price it paid for the debt and its face value. On the other hand, should a company eventually be com-pelled to seek bankruptcy protection, then Oaktree would be able to convert its discounted debt investment into a meaningful equity stake and potentially recast the bankrupt company's capital stack. Given a new lease on life with a capital stack more suited to the capabilities of its business model, the revived business would be able to embark on a new strategy to do what all highly successful businesses do: create EMVA.

Evolving Capital Choices

Bob Halliday, the founding chairman of our first public company, FFCA, made an observation about business that has stuck with me: "There are no new ideas in business; they just end up being repackaged in different ways." Well, I would like to think we've had a few firsts, but I basically agree with the observation. And I know for sure that ideas that involve adjusting the Six Variables that comprise business models are not patentable. Good ideas in finance end up being adopted and adapted, leaving little in the way of first-mover advantage to trailblazers.

With that said, OPM and OPM/equity sources, which comprise the essential tools for capital formation, do change. The OPM equity we accessed to start our first company was not available to start the second or third. The OPM equity we accessed to start our second public company was not available to start our first. And the OPM equity we accessed to start STORE Capital was unavailable to start either our first or second public companies. To give a nod to Bob Halliday, the actual capital *ideas* change little. But the *source* of capital is definitely subject to change.

When it comes to capital formation and capital stack tools, the business world has changed a great deal in my career. The emergence of investment management firms, which includes all manner of private equity investors and asset managers, is at the top of the list. These are precisely the kinds of companies that collectively dominate the business categories held by members of the 2021 Forbes 400 list of wealthiest Americans. Oaktree Capital, STORE's founding institutional shareholder, is one such company, and eventually gave rise to two members of the elite Forbes list. When I began my career in 1980, there were virtually no private capital firms. In the ensuing 40 years, thousands of such companies have emerged, with new entrants being added to the list every year. These firms include a mix of private equity, venture capital, distressed debt, and lending firms, amongst others.

The amount of private company investment capital that exists today adds to the dynamism of our economy and increases the chances for anyone to become engaged in business.

Given the abundance of private capital, corporate capital stacks that involve stock exchange listings have become less desirable over time. Between 2000 and 2019, the number of publicly listed companies declined by more than 38%.[2] In 2008, the number of companies held by private equity investors reached parity with the number of publicly listed firms. Ten years later, the number of privately held companies outnumbered publicly listed companies by nearly 75%. But here is a more telling statistic: Between 2005 and 2019, private equity firms outraised public IPOs by roughly 300%. During that same period, IPOs raked in a cumulative total of $610 billion, while share buybacks in the S&P 500 exceeded $7 trillion.[3]

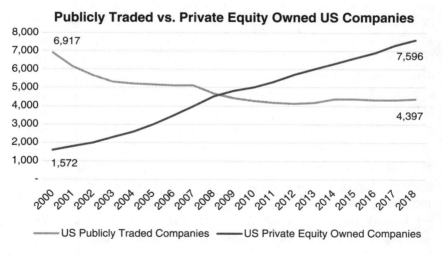

SOURCE: World Bank, World Federation of Exchanges, PitchBook, Credit Suisse. Data as of December 31, 2017, for listed companies and March 31, 2018, for private equity.

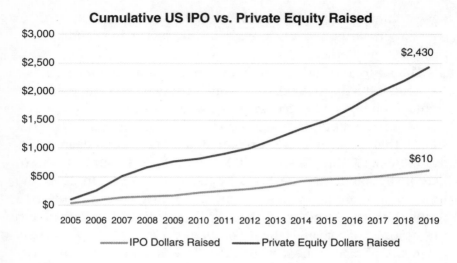

Cumulative US IPO vs. Private Equity Raised

SOURCE: Data from Statistica and Pitchbook

Of course, with OPM and OPM equity subject to change, 2021 would break this trend, delivering a record year for initial public offerings.[4] The surge in public company interest was propelled by low interest rates, high levels of investor liquidity and an appetite for emerging technologies having outsized growth potential. Consequentially, many of the newly introduced public companies possessed business models that were not thoroughly proven or defined. Driving more than half this IPO wave was the use of "blank check" companies whose purpose was to ease the simplicity of introducing private companies to the public markets. As a result, the net number of publicly traded companies did something it had not done in decades: increase. Meanwhile, private equity investments did not lose any of their luster, with assets under management and uninvested capital at or near record levels.

Just as the richest among us make for interesting study into the best business models of the ages, capital market changes deserve our attention because they reflect broader capital formation and capital stack trends that can impact the business community. In the public markets, there has been a distinct trend toward fewer companies, with investor sentiment favoring technology-driven growth companies. Meanwhile, the 10 largest companies by equity market capitalization in 2020 had grown to a high not seen since the dot-com boom, representing approximately 27% of the weighting of the S&P 500.

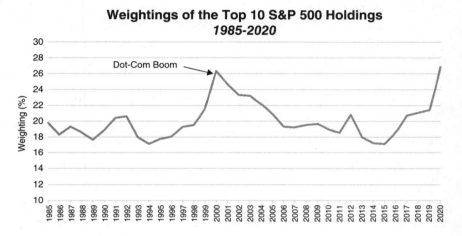

Weightings of the Top 10 S&P 500 Holdings
1985-2020

SOURCE: Data from Morningstar Direct

Value vs. Momentum Investing

Public stock trading patterns have meaningfully changed over my career, with the advent of commission-free trading platforms. Trading commissions used to impose frictional cost that limited trading activity. No longer is that true. During my tenure at STORE, we estimated that fully two thirds of the average daily trading in our shares was done by "day trading" investors who held on to our shares for mere minutes or hours. The growth in trading activity has had an undeniable impact on daily trading volume, which has the near-term potential to alter public company ownership and influence public market valuations.

Discount brokers are incentivized to encourage trading frequency, given that trading order flow comprises an important source of revenues. When opening my personal discount online brokerage account, I was interested to see what tools the various trading platforms offered that would allow me to evaluate my comparative investment performance. I wanted to know how I had done relative to the S&P 500 and other broad benchmarks. None of the online trading platforms I approached offered such performance evaluation tools. Knowing this gave me the sensation of being locked inside a Las Vegas casino having no windows or wall clocks that would allow me to know the time of day or the time spent gambling. The online trading firms did not want to help me understand how well I was doing at investing. "Buy and hold" value investment strategies, when viewed from the vantage point of discount brokerage firms, were less desirable. They simply wanted me to trade more.

In such a heady trading environment, long-term value investment strategies, which depend on fundamental corporate financial analysis and an understanding of equity return components, tend to be less in favor. After all, many of the day trades in STORE shares are placed by investors having little idea of what the company does, instead relying on trading algorithms that capture what they believe to be relevant relative value relationships. In this context, momentum can be important. I am not alone among business leaders in my counterintuitive observation that equity analyst "buy" recommendations tend to become far more frequent the higher the stock price.

With all this said, my observation is that, over the long term, corporate performance fundamentals win out. There is no long-term escape from the Six Variables of equity returns.

Value investing, which relies on an understanding of the Six Variables, may not be the dominant daily trading strategy of public company investors, but it still dominates.

For the millions of private companies and the entrepreneurs that found and lead them or the thousands of asset management firms that invest in them, value investing is generally all that matters.

Business investment components and operating cash flows enable OPM decisions.

The amount of cash flow left after paying for OPM enables YOM and OPM equity decisions.

And the sum of OPM, YOM, and OPM equity defines business valuation.

It's that simple.

Defining a Financial Win

Given the Six Variables underlying wealth creation, together with the fuel provided by compounding, what is a realistic aspirational financial win?

Over an 11-year period in the early part of my career and over 76 episodes, Robin Leach, an English entertainment reporter, had a successful syndicated television show called *Lifestyles of the Rich and Famous*, where he would highlight the palatial dwellings and extravagant trappings of the well-to-do. Shows like this, together with the annual attention drawn by the Forbes 400 and other media devoted to the flamboyantly wealthy, provide a misleading picture of what it means to be rich. The members of the Forbes 400 are not simply rich. They are extreme outliers beyond rational aspiration.

In 2020, there were estimated to be 927 billionaires in the United States out of a population of approximately 330 million people. Collectively, they controlled an estimated $3.7 trillion in assets, or an amount approximately equal to the annual gross domestic product of Germany, the world's fourth largest economy. Nearly 60% of the members of this group are self-made, and nearly all the fortunes in this group emanate from businesses boasting potent business models that have contributed meaningfully to our collective economic prosperity.

To live in a time where we can bear witness to significant amounts of wealth creation is historically rare and has had a positive impact on the majority of Americans. The revolutionary forces and capital formation that enabled the rise of the recently super-rich doubtless helped the careers of many businesspeople. When I started my career in 1980, there were likely fewer than 10 billionaires. Two years later, *Forbes* produced the first list of wealthiest Americans. The richest person on that list would not have even made their 2020 list. In fact, just one name on the 1982 list remained there through 2020. By 1987, the number of billionaires had risen fourfold to nearly 50, and the growth of the superrich has continued unabated since then.

When it comes to a realistic assessment of what constitutes personal wealth, it helps to take a step back. Just 10.4% of American households in 2019 had a net worth outside of their primary residence of more than $1 million. Realistically speaking, if you could be in this group, that would be a significant win. Just 1.2% of households had a net worth between $5 million and $25 million. And just 196,000 households, or about .2% of the total, had net worths in excess of $25 million. Buried somewhere in that last number are the nation's 927 unicorn billionaires.

Most importantly, and most concerning, roughly 64% of American households had a net worth less than $100,000 outside of their home, with much of that group having no savings. In fact, a survey conducted by GOBankingRates in June 2020 found that 40% of Americans aged 55 to 64 had no savings at all.

2019 US Household Wealth Distribution

Wealth Category[1]	(Thousands) Households	%
Less Than $100,000	78,284	63.7%
Mass Affluent ($100,000 – $1 Million)	31,800	25.9%
Millionaire ($1 Million – $5 Million)	11,000	9.0%
Ultra High Net Worth ($5 Million – $25 Million)	1,520	1.2%
$25 Million Plus	196	0.2%
Total	122,800	100.0%

[1] Wealth excludes primary residence.

SOURCE: Data from Spectrem Group, Market Insights 2020 United States Census Bureau

The median US household income in 2020 amounted to just below $70,000, with a median individual savings below $10,000. Indeed, the majority of Americans have little in the way of savings apart from Social Security and defined benefit pension plans, with the latter increasingly rare in corporate America.

2020 US Individual and Household Income Percentiles

	Percentile				
	25.0%	50.0%	75.0%	90.0%	99.0%
Individual Income	$23,000	$43,206	$75,050	$125,105	$361,020
Household Income	$34,301	$68,400	$123,580	$200,968	$531,020
Individual Savings	$0	$6,450	$96,000	$360,000	$1,770,500

SOURCE: Data from DQYDJ

Between June 2015 and December 2019, the average personal savings rate in the US approximated 7.4%, most of which was skewed toward the wealthiest households. At lower income levels, saving 7.4% of personal income can be difficult, if not impossible. The following table illustrates the lifetime savings that would be accumulated, assuming a 7% monthly savings rate and a 7% annual portfolio return. Given average actual 2020 individual savings at the 99th percentile of nearly $1.8 million and 75th percentile savings of under $100,000, it seems safe to say that computed retirement savings levels in the following table are likely to be more aspirational than real.

Household Accumulated Savings at 7% of Income

($000's)		Years of Savings				
		25	30	35	40	45
25th Percentile	$34	$162	$244	$360	$525	$759
50th Percentile	$68	$323	$487	$719	$1,047	$1,513
75th Percentile	$124	$584	$879	$1,298	$1,892	$2,734
90th Percentile	$201	$950	$1,430	$2,111	$3,077	$4,446
99th Percentile	$531	$2,509	$3,779	$5,579	$8,131	$11,748

Household Income

SOURCE: Data from DQYDJ

Saving for retirement is hard and requires a dedicated effort. It also takes a great deal of time. After 40 years of monthly savings of 7% of household income at a rate of 7%, those in the 90th percentile would have just over $3 million saved. In the 1990s, financial advisor William Bengen created the 4% rule of retirement withdrawal as a guidepost for safe pre-tax retirement income. That would mean that a retiree having $3 million saved could withdraw $150,000 annually, while a retiree having $500,000 saved could withdraw $25,000. Social Security and other retirement benefits would add to annual pre-tax post retirement earnings potential.

It can be daunting to think of the amount of retirement savings to assemble with a withdrawal limitation of just 4% annually. Yet, by 2021, given low prevailing interest rates and a stock market highly valued in historic terms, certain financial advisors began to openly talk about whether 4% might represent too aggressive an annual withdrawal target.

Given a reading of this book, together with an understanding of what it takes to accumulate $1 million over a lifetime of savings, it should come as no surprise that many of the wealthiest Americans accumulated their wealth a different way. They chose to be business owners and investors. They did not simply invest money that passively went to work for them, but invested in businesses they actively created and owned. Achieving a 7% compound annual portfolio rate of return can indeed make you rich, given a long enough runway and a high enough savings rate. However, owning or being a shareholder in a business capable of creating EMVA is a well-worn path to wealth exemplified by members of the Forbes 400 and widely practiced by entrepreneurs everywhere.

America is broadly in need of elevated financial literacy, which is part of the reason for this book and the STORE University video series that inspired it. At the corporate level, a win is not to harness the latest disruptive technology to create a global enterprise. The initial win is to try to make a decent living. The next level consumed much of this book: Making your company worth more than it cost. EMVA is wealth that is created from thin air, is something only companies can deliver, and is why the world's richest people generally have net worths sourced from personal business investments.

Corporate wealth creation requires a solid business model combined with the miracle of compounding, but the Six Variables of that model need not be perfect. Nor does the company have to address a large marketplace or be highly scalable. Meaningful wealth creation is possible with "old world" companies having numerous business model limitations. As to defining a "meaningful wealth" win, aiming for the 9% of American households having net worths between $1 million and $5 million seems an aspirational goal that is within reach. You are not likely to get on TV, own a jet, or buy a private island, but your economic achievement will have been noteworthy by any measure.

Some Final Thoughts

I personally know of no entrepreneurs who began their journeys with a personal wealth creation target. They simply harnessed what they were good at and applied that skill in the hope it would prove to be of value. In this sense, there exists a loose brother/sisterhood of entrepreneurs. For many of us, the businesses we have created and led enabled us to earn a living and save some money. As to business value creation, some of us failed to create wealth, others were able to create wealth, with a number of us landing a spot in the upper 10% of Americans having net worths greater than $1 million. Many of us have been on multiple entrepreneurial journeys where we have experienced successes and failures. But all of us appreciate what it takes to set up a successful business. The fine lines that separate entrepreneurs often come down to our diverse interests, the markets we work to address, and the problems our businesses are designed to solve.

When I left my first banking job in Atlanta to move to Arizona, I made a choice to devote my career to what I believed I was good at, which was finance. I also had a basic wealth aspiration that I might someday be a millionaire. Ultimately, I and others I work with did far better than we had anticipated. Importantly, our successes allowed us to make a positive difference in the lives of many others. Indeed, our journey is evidence that the art of the possible is always more than we initially believe to be possible.

To come full circle to where I started this book, our study of business within these pages is inextricably tied to the notion of wealth creation. How this all works, from a financial point of view, is not rocket science. My experience has been that good ideas for a business, coupled with business models that hold the promise of EMVA creation and good management teams to execute the plan, are scarcer than the financial capital needed to start them. My experience is that the opportunity to undertake such a business journey is nowhere more possible than right here in America. The dynamism of the American economy is what has enabled a country having just over 4% of the world's population to have approximately 30% of the world's wealth and roughly 16% of global gross domestic product at the end of 2019.[5]

In my opinion, equity returns lie at the center of the ability of the free enterprise system to outperform every other alternative. They are the prime determinant of OPM, equity OPM, business valuation, and equity market value added. They prompt capital allocation efficiency and direct attention to operating, asset, and capital efficiencies at the hands of business leadership. And the drivers of equity returns can be broken down into six simple, universal business model variables that collectively establish a framework for readily understanding how businesses work and create wealth that ultimately benefits us all.

Glossary of Terms

Asset efficiency   Improving a company's current equity return through a reduced business investment achieved by less invested in hard assets and a faster cash flow cycle.

Business investment   Cash assets at cost, less any non-interest-bearing obligations.

Capital efficiency   Improving a company's current equity return through capital stack adjustments that optimize OPM and equity use while limiting OPM payments and cost.

Capital stack   The various sources of capital used to finance business investment that bear a cost, including OPM, YOM, and OPM equity, used to finance a business investment.

Cash flow cycle   The time between the beginning of product creation and the collection of cash from the ultimate product sale. Slow cash flow cycles raise business investment through elevated inventory and accounts receivable levels.

Conglomerate   A company having diversified, unrelated business holdings.

Core competencies   Essential skills tethered to the problems and stakeholders that businesses are designed to address.

Cost of capital   The total annual OPM cost, together with the desired annual rate of return for equity investors shown as a percentage of the combined amount of OPM and equity.

EBITDA   Earnings before interest, taxes, depreciation, and amortization.

EBITDAR   Earnings before interest, taxes, depreciation, amortization, and rents on assets you could have otherwise purchased. This variable is generally preferable to EBITDA when computing the V-variable, because it is part of adding into business investment the estimated cost of rented assets that might otherwise have been purchased. By doing this, the estimated percentage of a company funded with OPM will be closer to the truth and the business fundamentals will be easier to compare to peer companies electing to own all of their assets. However, should you be unable to estimate such adjustments, electing to use EBITDA instead, the V-Formula result will turn out just the same.

Equity   Business investment less OPM.

Equity market value added (EMVA)   The amount by which the value of company equity exceeds the company equity investment at cost. Cost-based company equity investments include YOM, OPM equity, and free cash flows that are reinvested in the business.

Fixed-charge coverage ratio   EBITDAR divided by OPM payments. Here EBITDAR is computed before all rents (not just rents on asset you might otherwise have purchased) and OPM payments include all rents.

Maintenance capital expenditures (maintenance capex) Added business investment made each year to replace worn out assets, together with periodic business investments associated with asset refreshment essential to the maintenance of corporate revenues. To this, one can add periodic losses incurred from poor business investments made. While GAAP requires that research and development (R&D) costs be annually expensed as incurred, to the extent that R&D is expected to have lasting value, V-Formula adjustments are permissible. Operating profit margins can be increased by backing out lasting R&D costs, those costs can instead be added to business investment, with annual R&D maintenance costs included along with maintenance capex.

Market V-Formula   A formula to compute the current equity rates of returns for shareholders having acquired stock in a company for an amount different than the original cost of the equity.

Market value added (MVA)   The amount by which a company's enterprise value exceeds the cost of its creation. Beneficiaries of the value created include lenders and other OPM providers, together with equity investors, who are the prime beneficiaries of the value created.

Marginal Profits   The profits made on the last dollars of sales, which tend to be far higher than the profits made on the first dollars of sales as a result of business scalability.

Operating efficiency   Improving a company's current equity return through operating profit margin elevation achieved through higher sales, product pricing, or reduced operating costs.

Operating leverage   The ability of a company to grow revenues without adding to its business investment.

Operating profit margin   Earnings before interest, taxes, depreciation, amortization, other non-cash expenses and rents on assets you could own, but elect to rent shown as a percentage of revenues. Please note the acronym "OPM" is not used to describe operating profit margin.

OPM equity   Equity in a business that comes from other people.

Opportunity cost   The range of possible future business costs arising from decisions made today. Most often, business opportunity costs are associated with capital stack decisions.

Other people's money (OPM)   The amount a business borrows from third parties, plus the known cost of any assets the business elects to lease.

Payment constant   The sum of OPM payments divided into the amount of OPM obtained.

Scalability   The ability of a company to grow in size to address market opportunities. Scalability commonly accompanies higher marginal profitability where a sizable portion of a company's expenses are effectively fixed.

V-Formula   An equation to compute current corporate pre-tax equity returns.

Wealth creation multiple   The current equity rate of return as a multiple of required investor current equity rate of return.

Your own money (YOM)   Equity in a business coming out of your own pocket.

The Value Equation Framework

Current Pre-Tax Return on Equity

The V-Formula

(Sales ÷ Business Investment × Operating Profit Margin
− % of OPM × Rate Charged on OPM
− Annual Maintenance CapEx ÷ Business Investment

= Current Pre-Tax ROE
÷
% of Equity

This formula computes the current pre-tax return on equity of a business at cost.

The V-Formula Deconstructed

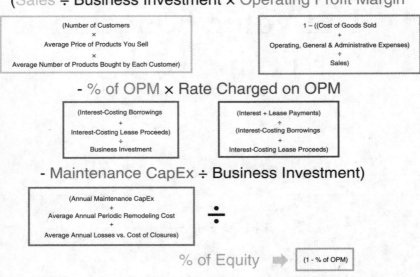

= Current Pre-Tax Return on Equity

The V-Formula can be expanded to include numerous potential variables.

Relative V-Formula for Current Pre-Tax Return on Equity

(Sales/Business Investment Ratio × Operating Profit Margin − % of OPM × Interest Rate − Annual Maintenance CapEx/Business Investment Ratio)

÷

% of Equity

The V-Formula can be viewed more basically as a series of relative numeric relationships.

Equity Valuation Multiple

> Your Current Equity Rate of Return
>
> ÷
>
> Required Investor Current Equity Return

This formula compares the current equity return your company can produce relative to the current rates of return other investors might find acceptable.

Equity Value

> Your Equity at Cost
>
> ×
>
> Equity Valuation Multiple

This formula calculates the estimated value of your company equity.

Equity Market Value Added (EMVA)

> Equity Value – Equity at Cost
>
> Or you can simply do as follows:
>
> (Equity Valuation Multiple – 1) × Equity Investment at Cost

This formula determines the amount of EMVA your company has been able to create.

Sustainable Growth Rate

(Sales ÷ Business Investment × Operating Profit Margin − % of OPM × OPM Payment Constant −Annual Maintenance CapEx ÷ Business Investment)
÷
% of Equity
×
(1 − The Tax Rate)

This formula determines how much the sales of your company can grow without needing new Equity or OPM Equity to help fund that growth.

Current Equity Rate of Return
With Partial Ownership

Your Company's Current Equity Rate of Return
×
Your Ownership%
÷
Your % of Equity Investment at Cost

This formula determines your personal current rate of equity return from your company at cost when you don't own all the equity.

Market Return on Equity

The Market V-Formula

(Sales ÷ (Business Investment + − EMVA) × Operating Profit Margin − % of OPM * × Interest Rate − Annual Maintenance CapEx ÷ (Business Investment + − EMVA))

÷

% of Equity *

*% of OPM and Equity are computed as a percent of Business Investment + − EMVA

This formula determines your current rate of equity return from an investment made at a market price in a public or private company that is either above or below the actual original cost of the company as adjusted by EMVA.

Company Valuation

((Operating Profits − Maintenance CapEx − OPM payments) ÷ Required Investor Current Pre-Tax Equity Return) + OPM

This formula illustrates how to value a company.

Compound EMVA Growth Formula

$$(Equity\ Market\ Value ÷ Equity\ at\ Cost)^{(1÷N)} − 1$$

Where N = Weighted average age of equity at cost

This formula, together with EMVA as a percentage of equity at cost, is a key measure of corporate value creation efficiency.

Notes

Chapter 1

1. 2021 Small Business Profile, US Small Business Administration Office of Advocacy.
2. Wealth-X's Billionaire Census 2021.
3. Wealth-X's Billionaire Census 2021.
4. Career money leaders list through February 2021, Professional Golf Association.
5. Dimitrije Curcic, "The Ultimate Analysis of NBA Salaries [1991–2019]," August 6, 2021, https://runrepeat.com/salary-analysis-in-the-nba-1991-2019.
6. 2020 Player Salaries, https://www.pro-football-reference.com/.

Chapter 2

1. J.D. Harrison, "When We Were Small: FUBU," *Washington Post*, October 7, 2014.

Chapter 3

1. In 1996, we created the first US real estate master trust. The idea was to borrow against a pool of real estate by issuing bonds. Then, later, we would grow the vehicle by adding pools of real estate in subsequent years. In this way, unlike traditional real estate bond issuance, where the bond holders are secured by the specific pool they invested in, master trust bondholders would be secured by the collective the real estate held in past and future pools. For investors, the disadvantage was that they would invest in a pool of notes secured by real estate, but without fully knowing what their ultimate collateral would look like, since we could add to and occasionally substitute the collateral. However, the clear advantage for investors was that the pool could grow larger and become far more diverse over time, with a resultant likelihood that it would perform consistently. By contrast, traditional individual pool borrowings could be expected to have a higher level of performance variability. For us, the master trust delivered secured vehicle where we could service and control our own assets, giving us the ability to sell, improve, or substitute real estate to maximize the value of the pooled assets. Alignments of interest are always important, especially since commercial real estate note issuances are done without recourse to the issuers. In our case, we had an equity commitment amounting to 30% of the real estate investment amount.

2. A present value is computed by discounting back future lease payments to be made at a company's estimated cost of borrowings to arrive at a theoretical borrowing equivalent. While the borrowing equivalent may be a reasonable approximation, the discounted value will not tend to equal the amount of OPM used, which is key in evaluating comparative corporate capital stacks. The present value of lease streams is also somewhat irrelevant, since companies nearly always extend leases or replace them with other leases. In that sense, computing the present value of a lease stream does not treat companies like going concerns. Financial statement analysts are most interested in the annual lease payment obligations and generally assume these to be ongoing or increasing, assuming the company is to remain the same size or grow.

Chapter 5

1. I introduced the V-Formula in the October 1999 issue of *Strategic Finance*, published by the Institute of Management Accountants. The article won the Lybrand Gold Medal for best manuscript of the year.

Chapter 6

1. Y-Charts and World Bank, World Federation of Exchanges Database.

2. Gary Fox, "FAANG—These Tech Giants = 10th Largest Economy in the World," May 4, 2020, https://www.garyfox.co/faang-stocks/.

3. "How Markets Work and the FAANG Mentality," Dimensional fund advisors using data from CRSP, November 1, 2019, https://www.dimensional.com/us-en/insights/how-markets-work-and-the-faang-mentality.

4. "How Markets Work and the FAANG Mentality," Dimensional fund advisors using data from Bloomberg LP, November 1, 2019, https://www.dimensional.com/us-en/insights/how-markets-work-and-the-faang-mentality.

Chapter 7

1. I introduced the notion of Six Shot Economics in the December 2007 issue of *Strategic Finance*, published by the Institute of Management Accountants.

Chapter 8

1. In our first two public companies, we were fortunate to have as a board member Shelby Yastrow, who had been personal counsel to Ray Kroc and for many years general counsel of McDonald's. He conveyed this story.

Chapter 10

1. Capitalism.com, "Aaron Dusted Off His Forgotten Invention and Turned It Into a 9-Figure Business," May 21, 2021, https://www.capitalism.com/scrub-daddy/.

Chapter 11

1. If you look closely at the chart and then look to the cash flow estimate of lost value, you may notice that they do not tie out. In fact, if one computes the cost of Walmart's balance sheet and equity each year and looks to the EMVA differences between 2001 and 2020, the loss in EMVA will approximate $130 billion, or more than $70 billion short of what the statement of cash flows would suggest. The difference principally lies in the company's large share repurchases, which were bought in at well above the underlying cost of those shares. Some differences may also arise from non-cash accounting asset impairments, which will obscure the degree of lost shareholder value by distorting the true cost of business investment. Cash flow statements rule, but the chart, taken from the company's fiscal year-end balance sheets, is still instructive.

Chapter 12

1. Center of Research in Security Prices, LLC.
2. Most of the historical facts were obtained from Lone Star Steakhouse & Saloon, Inc., History, http://www.fundinguniverse.com/company-histories/lone-star-steakhouse-saloon-inc-history/.
3. Funding Universe, Boston Market Corporation History, http://www.fundinguniverse.com/company-histories/boston-market-corporation-history/.
4. Louise Lee, "Worst One-Year Performer Boston Chicken Gets Booby Prize," *The Wall Street Journal*, February 25, 1998.

Chapter 13

1. Roger L. Martin, "M&A: The One Thing You Need to Get Right" (June 2018), *Harvard Business Review*.
2. Doug Olenick, "Apple iOS and Google Android Smartphone Market Share Flattening: IDC," *Forbes*, May 27, 2015.
3. Filmsite.org, The Pixar-Disney Animated Films, https://www.filmsite.org/pixaranimations.html.

4. Sarah Frier, "The Inside Story of How Facebook Acquired Instagram," August 4, 2020, OneZero.Medium.com.

5. Salvador Rodriguez, "As Calls Grow to Split Up Facebook, Employees Who Were There for the Instagram Acquisition Explain Why the Deal Happened," September 24, 2019, https://www.cnbc.com/2019/09/24/ facebook-bought-instagram-because-it-was-scared-of-twitter-and-google.html.

6. Rick Rothacker, "The Deal That Cost Bank of America $50 Billion – and Counting," *The Charlotte Observer*, August 17, 2014.

7. Tom Johnson, "That's AOL Folks," January 10, 2000, http://money .cnn.com/2000/01/10/deals/aol_warner/.

8. Rita Gunther McGrath, "15 Years Later, Lessons from the Failed AOL-Time Warner Merger," *Fortune*, January 10, 2015.

9. Thomas Gryta and Ted Mann, *Lights Out* (Houghton, Mifflin Harcourt, 2020).

10. Nicholas Gilmore, "The Forgotten History of How 1960s Conglomerates Derailed the American Dream," *The Saturday Evening Post,* November 1, 2018.

11. John Brooks, *The Go-Go Years: The Drama and Crashing Finale of Wall Street's Bullish 60s* (Allworth Press, 1973).

Chapter 14

1. Minda Zetlin, "Blockbuster Could Have Bought Netflix for $50 Million, but the CEO Thought It Was a Joke," *Inc. Magazine*, September 30, 2019.

2. History.com, "Apple Launches iTunes, Revolutionizing How People Consume Music," September 6, 2019, https://www.history.com/this-day-in-history/apple-launches-itunes.

3. Sherilyn Macale, "Apple Has Sold 300M iPods, Currently Holds 78% of the Music Player Market," October 4, 2011, thenextweb.com.

4. Linda Tucci, "Business Process Reengineering (BPR)," February 2018, https://searchcio.techtarget.com/definition/business-process-reengineering.

Chapter 15

1. The Sears & Roebuck Catalog, 1893–1993, Curio and Co.

2. The World Bank, World Federation of Exchanges Database.

3. S&P Global.

4. Corrie Driebusch, "IPO's Keep Jumping Higher. How Long Will the Ride Last?" *Wall Street Journal*, November 18, 2021.

5. Juan Carlos, ed., "All the World's Wealth in One Visual," January 16, 2020, https://howmuch.net/articles/distribution-worlds-wealth-2019; International Monetary Fund; World Bank.

Acknowledgments

This book has been nearly 25 years in the making, starting with the first company we took public in 1994 and then with its two successors, which we introduced to the public markets in 2004 and 2014. Throughout this three-decade journey, I was fortunate to work with and receive mentorship from a large team of leaders, starting with Mort Fleischer and his mentor, Bob Halliday. In the course of the extensive work and creativity entailed in business formation, I would often take time to write, setting down some of the earliest of my observations about business models, which formed the basis for this book. The earliest critiques I received came from the many leaders I have been fortunate to work with across our three successful companies who have been instrumental in inspiring me and helping me refine my thoughts.

I began to write this book following the onset of the global coronavirus pandemic in 2020. By the beginning of 2021, the book was starting to take shape and so I tested its content on a graduate student project workshop class I taught at Cornell University. Many of the initial edits and changes that came thereafter are owed to comments from my students and assistance from Associate Dean Alex Susskind. I was also grateful for the informative input I received from Amy Hillman and Tom Bates of Arizona State University. Paul Drake, Professor Emeritus of Physics at the University of Michigan, and a frequent contributor to Seeking Alpha, also added valuable input. Along the way, Thomas Hauck patiently edited the book twice. Brad Thomas, a fellow author and frequent writer on income-oriented investments, provided valuable input, as well as an appreciated introduction to my publisher, Wiley. Thanks also to Kevin Harreld, Susan Cerra and the entire team at Wiley for believing in this project and to my publicist, Jane Wesman, for helping me refine and deliver the final product. Bobi Seredich and EQ Inspirations worked their social media and presentational magic to improve the complete offering. Finally, as I wrote and tweaked the manuscript, I liberally submitted versions to friends, family members, securities analysts, investors, investment bankers, and university professors, as well as to STORE Capital team members and directors. To all of you who were so incredibly kind to immerse yourselves in this material, thank you! Your input has made me a better writer and this a better book.

About the Author

Beginning with his first job as a commercial banker in Atlanta, Georgia, Chris Volk formed an interest in corporate business models, financial statement analysis, and finance. From there, he moved to Arizona, where he would eventually guide the initial public listing and assume the presidency of his first real estate investment trust, a business that became a national leader in providing lease and mortgage financing solutions for restaurant and other chain store operators.

Over the next three decades, Chris was instrumental in founding and then publicly listing two other successful and market-leading net lease concerns. The most recent of these is STORE Capital, a company Chris guided for a decade as its founding chief executive officer through the beginning of 2021.

The business models of all three companies, backed by strong leadership teams, delivered attractive shareholder returns while benefiting a broad array of stakeholders. Altogether, Chris oversaw the successful deployment of more than $20 billion in net lease and mortgage capital to thousands of growing businesses across the United States.

Chris began to write about corporate finance early in his career, with articles covering subjects from financial statement analysis to business valuation and real estate investing. In 1999, he devised the Value Equation, or V-Formula, a simplified way to determine business equity returns. That year, he wrote an inaugural article that would go on to win the Lybrand Gold Medal, bestowed for the best article of the year by the Institute of Management Accountants. Later, Chris would write articles that expanded on his early V-Formula observations, culminating in an eventual award-winning video series that he created while chief executive officer at STORE Capital and which inspired this book. He was a 2019 regional winner of EY's Entrepreneur of The Year® award. He is a frequent lecturer to college and graduate students and serves on multiple charity boards. He resides with his wife in Paradise Valley, Arizona, and Huntsville, Alabama.

Index